The CH.

MW00454706

ISBN 9781698678832

THE CHAMELEON LEADER

CONNECTING WITH MILLENNIALS

Ranya Nehmeh

CONTENTS

PART I. MILLENNIALS – TOO BIG FOR THEIR BOX

PART II. THE SURVEY

PART III. THE CHAMELEON LEADER

PART IV. LIGHTS, CAMERA, ACTION

"A LITTLE KNOWLEDGE THAT ACTS IS WORTH INFINITELY MORE THAN MUCH KNOWLEDGE THAT IS IDLE."

- Khalil Gibran

MILLENNIALS -
TOO
BIG
FOR THEIR BOX

#MeetMaya

To other generations, it can really seem like millennials are from another planet sometimes. Consider the constant screen gazing, the matcha latte obsession, the job-hopping... you know what I'm talking about. I'm not a millennial. I'm a Gen Xer, more specifically a Xennial (no idea what these terms mean? Don't worry, we'll fill you in later in the book!), and an avid observer of how drastically things have changed in the workplace in the last few decades, especially in terms of leadership styles and theories.

In my position as a senior human resources professional, I often encounter millennials in the workplace and have more than once been frustrated by their apparent sense of entitlement and lack of commitment to their employers, and astonished when they just up and leave what I consider to be a promising job. And yet there has always been something about their approach that I admire.

Recently my extended family from the United States came to visit us in Vienna for the holidays and every evening, all ten of us would gather around the table, extra seating squeezed in, and share stories. One night, as we leaned back in our chairs, picking aimlessly at the remaining snacks on the table, the conversation drifted into work and jobs. My younger cousin Maya, in her early 20s, had recently started her first job, after graduating with an undergraduate degree in international relations. She was holding court and complaining to all of us about her current supervisor; he was old (in her books, old referred to someone in their 50s), he was not knowledgeable, was demotivating, and did not trust her to do anything right. This ancient man had no idea how to use technology, and he NEVER listened to her. "How should I learn anything from him?" she said, exasperated. On and on, the complaining went. She continued to explain her frustrations with her boss and was occasionally interrupted by someone throwing in comments like "Welcome to the real world", or "Just be happy that you have a job that pays your rent".

Similar thoughts were going through my mind, but after several years of conscious self-reflecting and forcing myself to think outside the box, I decided to challenge the voice in my head that was relying on an "imprinted dialogue", and really listen to Maya without judgment.

What I came away with was that depending on age, people had different expectations of the workplace. Around this kitchen table, we had a variety of generations spouting their opinions, and most of them seemed intent on telling Maya how things were, and advising that she just needed to accept the status quo. Clearly annoyed, she said:

"It's not like there is only one way to do things, and besides, the world has changed a lot! You all seem very threatened by young people."

There I had it, in a nutshell. The world has changed a lot. Technology has evolved so rapidly in the last decade that we are barely keeping up. Artificial intelligence is threatening jobs. Ghosting is a thing. Networks are huge and impersonal thanks to social media.

Most millennials didn't witness this change the same way the rest of us did; the younger ones were born into it. Many don't have memories of life before the Internet. Their world has always had a bigger reach than ours.

The concept of generational differences in the workplace is not new to me. I have read extensively on the topic and have always taken a special interest in workplace dynamics. I felt this generation gap when I started my first job years ago. However, what Maya was alluding to is much bigger than that. The duality of expectation versus reality in the workplace was causing her to feel disillusioned. She had gone from an energetic, excited university graduate to an uninspired employee faster than a viral video.

I could relate. Fifteen years ago, that had been me. During my first job, after receiving my postgraduate degree, I had felt super-confident and knowledgeable. I had been so ambitious, ready to take on new challenges and responsibility, prepared to make a difference in the workplace, and above all I wanted to be inspired and led by my supervisors. But no one listened to me at work, because I was considered young and inexperienced. I had faced similar disappointments to what Maya was describing, but slowly, I came to accept it and adapted myself to the workplace and now I am very comfortable in my mid-management career.

However, here is the problem. Maya's generation is bolder, hungrier to play a significant role in the company, much more demanding of what they think they're entitled to and they don't believe in limitations or inequalities. And the job market is becoming increasingly less stable. Think fight or flight.

> Millennials are often accused of having an "entitlement complex", which is the belief that they are owed something intrinsically, whether it's participation trophies in school, higher salaries or promotions in the workplace, quick and easy access to the Internet, and voicing their opinions and thoughts when they don't get these things immediately. A study by the University of Hampshire even highlighted that millennials scored 25 per cent higher in entitlement-related issues than their 40-60 year old counterparts (Generation X) and 50 per cent higher than those over 60 (Baby Boomers). The score was calculated based on questions that reveal attitudes of entitlement, such as probing whether participants felt they deserved certain things, or asking how superior they felt to others (Alton, Larry, 2017).

I had been quiet for several minutes, listening to what was unfolding, and then when Maya's comment silenced the table and others were busy rolling their eyes, shaking their heads, and making the tsk-tsk sound of disapproval, I spoke.

"What would make you happier at work? How do you want your supervisor to lead you?"

She took a few seconds to think about it, and when she answered, I knew I had hit the nail on the head: her tone softened, her demeanour became more open and relaxed. She was pleased to be asked for her opinion. She spoke at length about what she expected from a supervisor: characteristics, habits, and communication style. It made sense and did not sound like the ranting of a naïve and immature millennial. In the back of my mind, I heard the mutterings of somewhat unnecessary demands: cafeteria with specialist coffee baristas, music by rapper Drake playing in the common working areas, a ping-pong table in the workplace and those bean bag chairs that hipster start-ups scatter to encourage creative thoughts. However, she didn't want any of these things including freaking bean bag chairs; she wanted a career. She wanted to be heard. She wanted to know that her opinion mattered. She wanted to be inspired.

It's so easy to dismiss this generation as entitled, rolling our eyes and sighing at their boldness. It wasn't Maya's fault that she was rewarded for every little thing she did at school or grew up with a spoon-fed parenting style; she wasn't to blame for being part of the digital world, or being able to post a pic, write a quirky caption, WhatsApp a friend and check the latest Instagram feed in a matter of seconds. She was dealing with the world that was handed to her. What we are expecting from this generation is based on the way we experienced life and work.

But... believe it or not...the world has changed.

There is a vast amount of writing on leadership, and today's leader looks very different from leaders of past decades. Leading in this age of technology and social media requires a different approach. Most of the books I read on leadership are written by professionals in a particular field, experts who have years of experience, or highly successful CEOs with their own unique approaches on how to lead. We are living in an age of constantly changing technology, innovation, mass consumerism and instant gratification. The world is moving at such a fast pace that sometimes even I, who pride myself on being tech-savvy, can't keep up with the latest technological advances and social media trends. By the time I got around to using Snapchat, it had already become a thing of the past.

So how does one learn how to best lead in this time of unrelenting momentum? After listening to Maya, I realised I needed to mingle with young people, online and face-to-face. If we want to know how to lead millennials, we need to ask them what they want.

And so, after dozens of conversations, a few too many matcha lattes, and hundreds of survey responses, this book was created to answer the question:

"Hey, millennials, what do you need from your supervisors to feel inspired in the workplace?"

More specifically:

- Describe your ideal supervisor?

- What traits and qualities should this leader possess?

Some of you may be thinking, "Who cares what they want? They need to toughen up, adapt." Anyone who knows anything about leadership knows that the best leaders inspire. People are more productive when they feel motivated to come to work, when they care about the product, service, or people in their workplace, and when they think they are making a difference or a contribution.

I spent hour upon hour researching answers to these questions. During this time, I talked to hundreds of millennials to gain some insight into their needs and expectations about the leader they felt would best motivate and inspire. Most of the data collected came from an online questionnaire, and some through formal and informal meetings, over coffee or drinks, in conferences or in cafes. It didn't matter where, because in the end, what was important was that they had something to say and someone to listen. Their answers were innovative, creative, inspirational, smart, determined, rational, and knowledgeable.

As you will see, the basis of this book is a survey I conducted with over 700 millennials from around the world. When I first started jotting down notes for the book, still in the ideas phase, my plan was to create an awareness that millennials are somehow misunderstood and perhaps we can offer them more in order to get great results in the workplace. However, as the data started flowing in, I became aware that there was consistency in what they were asking for. It wasn't so much that they were misunderstood, it was more that they wanted a leadership style that was in sync with the times (technology, social media, ethics, respect), that catered to their perspective and strengths. Leadership is a huge subject with massive amounts of theorising that has gone through many changes over the decades.

From the survey data, I was able to create a leadership model that I called "The Chameleon". I will go into more detail in Part III, but essentially the model highlights the various qualities that an ideal leader of millennials would possess. Why a chameleon? Because chameleons change colour according to the situation. They are adaptable!

My goal is that this book will become a manual for leaders who are ready to embrace this young and ambitious generation and lead them energetically into the future. This will require a shift in mind-set, a visionary approach, a willingness to collaborate not dictate, inspire not conspire, but most importantly to get excited about the potential benefits of having this generation on board.

#WhyWeShouldCare

Talking down about millennials has become a way for the rest of us to vent our anger about the workplace and the long list of things that are wrong, regardless of the field or industry. Let's face it: As a society, for the most part, we think it is okay to comment and criticise. We do it with celebrities, with fashion, with lifestyle, and have a huge playing field with which to make our thoughts known.

Demographics are important for understanding social factors, and crucial to sales and marketing success. However, they also provide an easy way to classify someone according to some very general criteria. We need to avoid thinking that so-and-so is the way he is because he's a millennial and then walking away with nothing learned. The information is meant to give us an impression and better understanding of why a group is unique based on their social influences.

So back to #whyweshouldcare (how to lead millennials). We should care so that we are open-minded, and aware that this age group has a lot to offer. We should care so that we stop criticising, and start listening. We should care because, as cliché as it sounds, these guys are the future, so we kind of need to understand where they are taking us.

The field of leadership is vast, consisting of a multitude of theories and practices, models, and hypotheses.

When I first started learning about leadership in university, as part of my undergraduate business degree, I studied transactional leadership theories, transformational leadership theories and countless more. This was in the late 1990s; many students didn't even own laptops and had to use university computers to complete their assignments. Mobile phones were still not the norm, and there was no Google or social media. I sent my first email during my first year at university in 1996. Needless to say, the world was a very different place back then, as was the working environment.

Even though the more traditional approaches and theories are important in order to understand the progression of this field and have a holistic approach, concepts of leadership have developed.

However, the one constant over the last decade in the workplace has been that of fast-paced change. In order to keep up with this pace, leaders need to be open to different ways of thinking, new strategies and ways to inspire and motivate people, especially the younger workforce.

There is so much literature about leadership; you can read about it in articles, magazines, books, blogs, social media (the Instagram hashtag for leadership is over 9.9 million) or hear about it on podcasts. As a result of all this information, we can now access a lot of thorough and comprehensive ideas and studies about leadership with the click of a button. This is one of the beauties of technology. But the flip side is that there is also too much information available. If you search for an overview on leadership, you would soon be overwhelmed. And most of the information is similar in content: the importance of good leadership skills for the workplace, how to foster these skills, what characteristics make a good leader, the challenges of good leadership and so on and so forth.

So the key is to stop trying to lead millennials by using generic leadership approaches, and start looking for innovative ideas that speak to this specific target group, because times have changed, and generic just doesn't make the cut.

#WhatYouWillGainFromThisBook

This book aims to:

- **Show you that regardless of your position or title, you can be a great leader to the millennials in the workplace**

- **Explore what leaders can do to inspire millennials and reap the rewards**

- **View the millennials in a positive light and be open to their contributions, and not obsess over their faults**

A big YES of this book is the notion that anyone can inspire and lead. By that, I certainly don't mean that we all have what it takes to be the next Gandhi or Martin Luther King Jr., but when it comes to the workplace, you can be a leader.

This is as valid for senior management who oversee scores of large teams, mid-management who may only have one person working for them, or staff who manage NO ONE. How so, you may ask? A book I read years ago, *The Leader Who Had No Title: A Modern Fable on Real Success in Business and in Life*, by Canadian writer and motivational speaker Robin Sharma, reinforces the concept that one doesn't need to have a title to be a leader. The traditional path has always been that in order to become a leader, you need to work your way up the company ladder to get that particular title or position, but this book suggests that the founding principle is that of self-leadership, and that anyone who understands this can lead regardless of their official title within the organisation.

According to Sharma, the deeper the relationships you forge, the stronger your leadership skills. One of my favourite quotes from his book is:

"Leave every single person who intersects your path better, happier, and more engaged than you found them."

It is not the title that deserves respect but the contribution you make to your work and relationships.

At a leadership workshop organised by the Cornell SC Johnson College of Business, Cornell University, one of my colleagues mentioned to the facilitator that she did not feel that she was in a position of power to influence the senior management in our organisation. The facilitator's answer has resonated with me ever since.

> *"Everyone always has some kind of influence, if it's not upwards, then it's lateral with other peers and colleagues, and if not lateral, then with the staff who are reporting to you. Either way, by influencing just one person, you can cause a ripple effect."*

This advice brought me straight back to Sharma's book. If everyone can practise self-leadership in the workplace, then any of us have the power to influence, motivate, and inspire. And by doing that, we may be sparing millennials those first pangs of professional disillusionment that many of them experience in the early stages of their careers.

#StopCriticisingStartLeading

This book focuses on Generation Y (Gen-Y), otherwise known as millennials. Based on the work of historians Strauss and Howe who coined this term in their book, *Generations: The History of America's Future, 1584 to 2069*, millennials are the generation born between 1980–2000. This is an approximate date, which may vary slightly depending on the source being used. In 2019 the people in this age bracket would be between 19–39 years of age. Generalising this group, as we do for the Traditionalists (born 1922–1945), Baby Boomers (born 1946–1964), and Generation X (born 1965–1980) enables us to observe trends based on shared experiences and common perspectives.

Demographic labelling obviously has advantages, mostly to anyone marketing or selling something, but it is still a way of categorising people and trying to fit them into a box. And we all know that a one-size box does not fit all! Many of the millennials I have spoken to detest the idea that they aren't seen as original. Or perhaps they are more upset about the negative criticism the characteristics used to describe this particular group has resulted in.

> *"We are criticised so often by others in the workplace, mainly by the older generations, and yet we show up, and we produce results. Maybe our methods are different but that's not to say that they are inefficient. Ultimately, most people fear change and they are scared of what they don't know. And they let it out on us."*
>
> *Alexander, 30*

A New York Times article (2013) questioned the validity of stereotypes regarding this generation and went so far as to suggest they were, in fact, a much more homogenous group than indicated initially. This article was then the basis for a study conducted by Glocalities (Flash Report: The disruptive mind set of millennials around the globe, 2014) that tried to determine whether they are indeed the most globalised and connected generation ever (with similar values and behaviours around the world) or whether the picture is more fractured (diverging values and behaviour). The results indicated that they are both at the same time. They came up with five types of millennials based on values shaped by people and society.

CHALLENGERS

Competitive workers with a fascination for money, risk, and adventure

CONSERVATIVES

Family people who value tradition, etiquette and structure

SOCIALISERS

Structure seekers who enjoy entertainment, freedom, and family values

CREATIVES

Open-minded idealists who value personal development and culture

ACHIEVERS

Entrepreneurial networkers who value family and community

It's a fascinating study, but one that I believe also begs the question: What difference is there really, between segmenting millennials from one category to five? They are still being labelled, and perhaps, in this case, they are being put in even narrower boxes. And why can't these same segments be applied to the other generations?

And what about the 20-year age range of millennials? In the workplace, my 37-year-old colleague, who is still considered a millennial, exhibits completely different traits, expectations, and characteristics than the 24-year-old millennials that we have recently recruited. Needless to say, their various needs in the workplace are based on life experience and rank, but core expectations seem to be shockingly different. How do 15 years of technological advancement change and influence people? Technology is one of the most significant differentiating factors for millennials.

Accordingly, people born in the first years of the 1980s would not have grown up using laptops and mobile phones for most of their childhood. These only became readily available when they were nearing university; whereas those millennials who are now in their early 20s grew up with high-speed Wi-Fi, Facebook, Google, smartphones, social media apps, and an intensified expectation of instant gratification, from Tinder to Amazon. This seems to have transferred to real-life expectations, blurring the lines between what technology can deliver and what people, organisations, and experiences can deliver. This level of technology, hyperconnectivity, and access would have been unimaginable for those who were teenagers in the '90s. So how can they possibly share similar characteristics when their whole view of the world has been shaped differently? Older millennials were swayed by old-school ideas and technology that was still in its formative years. When technology boomed, they were well into their 20s. Think of yourself at 25, experiencing something for the first time. The level of excitement is huge, as opposed to the cool "been there, done that" attitude of the younger ones who were well adapted by this age. It is therefore not uncommon that micro-generations within the millennials have sprung up.

As someone born in 1978, I have an interesting position, because I am relatively close in age to an older millennial, yet based on the actual definition, I am a Gen Xer. But because no category will go undefined by academics and marketers, let us consider the Xennials - those born between 1977 and 1985. I know, the term sounds a bit otherworldly, perhaps a sci-fi film starring Ashton Kutcher and Mila Kunis. I only stumbled upon this definition by chance. It's a term coined by Sarah Stankorb and Jed Oelbaum in the online magazine Good ("Reasonable People Disagree about the Post-Gen X, Pre-Millennial generation", 2014). The article describes this generational group, which is in-between Gen X and millennials, or as they have referred to it "a micro-generation that serves as a bridge between the disaffection of Gen X and the blithe optimism of Millennials." This generation is old enough to have lived a childhood free of the internet but young enough to have spent their working lives online.

One of the main differences Stankorb points out is that many Xennials made it through their childhood and teen years without social media; they generally did not get cell phones until their 20s and grew up with payphones and landlines. They aren't especially pessimistic but are certainly not as optimistic and confident as the millennials. They are referred to as the "lucky" generation because they missed out on some of the global misfortunes that the generations before and after them experienced. When the 2008 recession hit, the Xennials were already in the workforce, whereas many millennials were just graduating and looking for employment, so there was a lot of disillusionment. They were still young when the market crashed and hadn't invested much, nor did they lose homes or retirement savings, unlike many Gen Xers. Adding the Xennial generation to the mix gives us a more realistic and accurate perspective. It also narrows the definition of millennials to a 15-year age gap. This book, therefore, takes the view that millennials are those people born 1985 to 2000, who would now be between 19 to 34 years of age.

#BottomsUpApproach

Don't rely on traditional approaches to leadership. These have typically been influenced by top-down leadership, where there may or may not be a transparent chain of command. Successful leaders in the workplace are, of course, in an excellent position to share their considerable knowledge of good leadership practices in addition to the characteristics and traits of effective leadership. However, given the millennials in the workplace and the changing working attitudes, this approach may not embrace their full potential, because it doesn't include the millennial perspective.

And the millennial perspective is highly unique.

According to our surveyed millennials, it is really important to them to be included in the process. This means being given the opportunity to express their opinions and views, provide insight and feedback, and be valuable members of the team.

This is the bottoms-up approach. It is collaborative, open, and transparent.

It also assumes equality regardless of title or position, and that each member is essential and valued. Listening to what the millennials want will enable us to draw from a variety of ideas rather than having policies and commands dictated from the top levels, people who are often quite isolated and out of touch to what's happening at the other levels of the organisation.

Involving millennials in the leadership process is also a means to convey to them that there is a shared responsibility in leading within a workplace and that they are part of it. It encourages a sense of ownership and creates more loyalty, engagement, and motivation because they feel they are valued. This bottoms-up approach also reduces the "them and us" generation gap that is so typically found in organisations, which tends to leave millennials feeling misunderstood and frustrated.

#Millennialism

Millennials account for roughly 27 per cent of the global population, or about 2 billion people globally (Pew Research Center, July 2018). As I mentioned, there are definitely cultural variances, but understanding their world, what influences them, and how they react is key to developing a leadership style that is inclusive, inspiring, and speaks their language. Be prepared to be surprised. Your automatic response might be that they probably respond best to technology, the shorter the communication the better - heck, let's just send them a photo and call it a day. Not the case. Millennials appreciate communication!

Characteristics & Traits

Some of the characteristics exhibited by this generation are conflicting. On the one hand, millennials are open-minded, confident, self-expressive, upbeat, liberal, and receptive to new ideas and new ways of doing things. On the other hand, they have also been coined the "Me Me Me Generation" - very focused on themselves, self-centred, almost narcissistic (ouch!). They are achievement oriented and passionate, yet at the same time, they are criticised for not being committed to their jobs. They are notorious for job-hopping and ghosting employers. I had heard of people ghosting each other after one or two dates (literally disappearing, not returning calls or texts, with no explanation) but to do this in the workplace seems somehow more reprehensible because it shows a blatant disregard for their own careers. Why so laissez faire?

According to the 2018 Deloitte Millennial Survey, 43 per cent of millennials envisioned leaving their jobs within two years; and only 28 per cent sought to stay beyond five years.

They are also known to be multi-taskers, but concurrently are accused of being lazy. They are often portrayed as naïve, especially in financial literacy, yet so many of the most successful companies today were started by millennials: Mark Zuckerberg, founder of Facebook; Andrew Mason, founder of Groupon; Kevin Systrom and Mike Krieger, co-founders of Instagram; Drew Houston and Arash Ferdowsi, cofounders of Dropbox; to name just a few. Even in the world sphere, they have made their mark: Malala Yousafzai, a Pakistani activist, was the youngest person to receive the Nobel Peace Prize for her work advocating for public education for all children. The millennials are also the generation re-creating their industries. Take blogging as an example. At its most basic, blogging is a free way to provide online content, but over the last ten years, it has been transformed into a profession in its own right. Millennials create opportunities through blogging. Successful bloggers that can attract a substantial following earn power, become influencers, and can make a lot of money. Millennials who started simple blogs, like Italian Chiara Ferragni with The Blonde Salad, or Sophia Amoruso who launched the retail website, Nasty Gal, selling vintage clothing, both at 22 years old, are now hailed as important businesswomen and powerful "digital influencers".

Who are the millennial game changers? TIME magazine's May 2018 issue headlined ten millennials who are reshaping music, sports, fashion, politics, and the environment. Among them, pop singer Ariana Grande, American football star Chris Long, and fashion's new face, Ghanaian model Adwoa Aboah. And let's not forget the likes of Queen B (Beyoncé). The common traits they exhibit are confidence, ambition, eagerness, enthusiasm, showing no limitations as to what they can achieve, and above all wanting to effect change. They are also dedicating themselves to global social causes, whether it is in support of children's education, opening up NGOs or talking about mental health and sexuality. It's not a new thing to use your fame to help a cause, because let's face it, people respond to famous people. However, this generation isn't about being the "poster boy/girl", it is about reaching vast numbers of people through social media, and spreading not just a message but also a perspective. They aren't about slogans; they are about connecting people.

Social media can be very inclusive, allowing people to find their tribes.

Millennials are also the generation known to be more racially diverse and more educated, yet shaking up social structures by delaying marriage and kids, which inevitably has a great impact on the workplace. A lot of the motivation of previous generations was to work hard, to gain financial stability and then to own things - a house, a car, another vacation home, luxury goods - owning beautiful things was the pinnacle of their success. However, the millennials are more about access than ownership. Huge companies such as Airbnb, Uber, and Car2Go have all made their success based on this phenomena: by providing products and services without the burdens of ownership, giving rise to what is now being called the "sharing economy" (Goldman Sachs Global Investment Research, 2018). This is reinforced by Jeremy Rifkin, author and economist, who comments that "25 years from now, car sharing will be the norm, and car ownership an anomaly". For the millennials, the experience is the new status symbol trumping ownership.

Most notably, millennials are the tech-savvy generation; no doubt about it, they are used to getting instant access to information. In fact, most of them have never had a world without "on demand" access. It's not surprising then that their obsession and attachment with mobile phones is as great as their need to publicise their lives online. There tends to be so much annoyance and irritation from previous generations about millennials and their phones, but we now understand that it's a dopamine addiction. Every time the phone beeps with a message or a new "like", we get a rush of dopamine, a cheap thrill because we feel connected, and seen.

Social media is a way to choreograph our lives, to control how we wish to be seen, but as a result we open ourselves up to being judged, which causes a chain reaction of self-reflection.

Millennials may have a need to be authentic, but they still need to check in with social media to make sure they are doing 'authentic' right.

If anything is to blame, it's technology. Also, if the world had been that interconnected 30 years ago, who's to say that the baby boomers would not have acted in exactly the same way? I could totally imagine my mother uploading one too many pictures on Facebook or Instagram at whopping speed.

The truth is that the digital revolution has changed the way we operate and has made this generation very unique. In the TED talk by millennial Jared Kleinert, he says that never before have young people had so much power to change the world. They can learn about everything they are passionate about almost instantaneously; this hyperconnectivity has made them so open-minded about events around the world and it's given them more power than ever before. They grew up with this knowledge and belief. It's not a new concept to them. We see it everywhere. Social media plays a huge role in raising global awareness, for example during the Arab Spring in 2010, and it was just the beginning for a new vehicle of activism. You no longer need to own or work at a network to spread news - one tweet or hashtag can now create global movements, i.e. #blacklivesmatter, #MeToo, #jesuischarlie, #refugeeswelcome, #lovewins. The power balance has been tipped. Again, you don't need to be a leader to have power. To quote Ian Somerhalder, actor and entrepreneur, from the Social Good Summit in 2017:

> **"Millennials don't just want to read the news anymore. They want to know what they can do about it."**

Perhaps this is a natural reaction to the overload of information we receive on a daily basis. It makes us feel helpless, so we do what we know how to do, and in the case of millennials, this is social media.

When millennials dislike something, it can have major global repercussions. One of the best examples is from Proctor & Gamble, whose fabric softener sales plummeted by 25 per cent over the last decade because millennials simply don't buy it (July 2018). Proctor & Gamble claims that millennials don't know what the product is for, but the more feasible explanation is that they are more eco-conscious than their parents' generation and therefore don't want to use too many toxic chemicals in their homes.

Why Do We Love to Hate On Millennials?

I think the simple answer to this question is that we fear what we don't understand, and hate stems from fear. And yes, hate is a ridiculously strong word to use here. This particular group seems to get a lot of media attention and criticism so perhaps we feel well informed to judge and react.

They do have a certain sense of entitlement, a "the world is my oyster" attitude. Here's the deal: In every generation there are pros and cons; things we like, others we dislike. But there are facts one cannot deny. Millennials have so many more opportunities than previous generations ever did. And yet the only certainty in the working world is uncertainty. That's a lot to handle. Especially when your parents were likely baby boomers - you know who you are! The generation that received student grants, graduated and had their choice of jobs, only knew what they read in the newspapers and saw with their own eyes, which in turn gave them a fairly limited view of the world.

So if the times that millennials are growing up in makes them a little selfish (translation: self-protective) and individualistic by nature, then so be it. These same traits are also hailed as being positive in the workplace: their healthy confidence should be admired, not seen as a negative trait. The job market doesn't provide the job security that it used to. Many university graduates can't find work, education has become increasingly expensive, and some would say a business serving its own needs. Young millennials work as unpaid interns just to get their foot in the door, or gain some experience.

So why is job-hopping criticised? Studies have shown that millennials don't job-hop any more than Gen Xers. Perhaps millennials are a much hotter subject in the media, much more under the microscope because of social media so we think they move around more because we talk about it more. Or perhaps it's the way they do it – just up and leaving with very little, if any, notice. Remember this is a generation that doesn't take things lying down. They have strong values and are idealistic in many ways. The pace of life has increased for all of us, which translates to: Why waste time doing something that has no benefit?

And we can't ignore the fact that the job market is much more volatile than it was only decades ago. Jobs are being replaced by robots and artificial intelligence; new types of jobs that we couldn't even imagine ten years ago are being created. This era of stability in the workplace is ending. So the reason that millennials leave one job after a short time might be to gain skills and find a place, even short-term, where they feel valued and appreciated. If we swivel our head and focus on the employer and not the employee, we will notice that millennials are not being offered job security, opportunities to grow, a challenging position, or appreciation the way employees were decades ago, so this attitude of looking after their own needs first is one of survival.

And it takes guts to leave a job, either for another one or to pursue something different. At a TED-curated event, millennial Daniela Zamudio said,

"I'm a quitter and I'm very good at it."

She was referring to the multiple jobs, cities, schools, studies and relationships she has quit, which in her view is not seen as a sign of weakness, laziness or being uncommitted. Instead, she argues that leaving one path to follow another is a sign of strength and often leads to greater happiness in the long run. She refers to the notion of "conscious quitting", which is having a strategy in place and weighing the pros and cons of quitting a particular situation, which is different than quitting without a plan.

Maslow's Millennials

When I was in university in 1996, I studied Maslow's hierarchy of needs, which was a theory he proposed in his 1943 paper "*A Theory of Human Motivation*". I was fascinated. Imagine a five-level pyramid explaining human behaviour in terms of what motivates us. Beginning with the lowest level: *physiological* (food, water, rest), *security* (the need for safety, shelter, stability), *social* (the need for friendship, love, belonging), to the more complex ones: *ego* (the need for self-esteem, power, recognition), and the highest need at the top of the pyramid, *self-actualisation* (the need to fulfil our potential development and creativity). Accordingly, Maslow proposed that we must satisfy the lower level (survival) needs before we can fulfil the upper level (growth) needs.

This model received some criticism, mainly because it could not be empirically tested, but at the same time it provided a useful summary of what makes humans feel satisfied in life. A new version of Maslow's hierarchy of needs was developed by Bauer Media based on millennial behaviour. Over 3,000 participants in the UK responded to create their own hierarchy of needs. As a result, five categories emerged based on their input: *The Influencers, The Adopters, The Apprentices, The Entertained* and *The Contented*. The different segments generated distinct hierarchy pyramids, as shown on the next page.

THE INFLUENCERS	THE ADOPTERS	THE APPRENTICES	THE ENTERTAINED	THE CONTENTED
Living life to the max! Career based on a personal passion	Strong desire to achieve, but wary of failure	Want to feel they're striving and achieving	Want a job they love	Not driven to seek the next career challenge
Peer respect via good career and looking good	Validation and reassurance of worth and skills	Being happy in themselves	Strive to be the best they can, high self-esteem	Esteem highest when in their comfort zone
Having (only) good friends. Being an advice giver	Best friends – support network and sounding board	Support & inspiration from family and friends	Meaningful relationships with family and friends	Settled and started/ looking to start a family
Being financially secure	Accommodation, job	Home – cherish having a solid base	Knowing your family are safe and well	Home is a safe haven, important for familiarity & decompression
Smartphone / laptop! Need access to friends and info at all times	Sometimes compromise the basics (food, sleep) for other steps on the pyramid (friends, work)	Being healthy is good for happiness	Sleep is great but sometimes they don't get enough	Healthy food and lots of water

For *The Influencers*, their physiological needs include the basics, such as food and water, but also their smartphone or laptop, as these are the main ways they access the internet. They need to be connected at all times, whereas self-actualisation for them is about living life to the fullest in all parts of their life, including their careers. On the other hand, *The Apprentices* listed health as their physiological need for happiness and their self-actualisation is to feel they are striving and achieving. They are more focused on just being happy with what they have at that moment, not necessarily because of the objects they have in their life, which is very much in line with the need for access over ownership. This revised version of Maslow's hierarchy clearly indicates the complexities of this generation, and understanding their needs and wants is the first step towards building working relationships with them.

#MindTheGap

Remember Maya, my disillusioned cousin? Well, as it turns out, she is not an isolated case. The more millennials I spoke to, the more I realised that this dissatisfaction with supervisors and the workplace in general is quite a common phenomenon.

The theme that came up over and over again, in my conversations, and in the survey results was that of *EXPECTATIONS*, or rather *UNMET EXPECTATIONS*. We have all been in situations where our expectation fell short of reality, whether in relationships, jobs, travel, going to the gym. However, it seems that the millennials experience this much more often. Curious, right? This might suggest that their expectations are too high, or that reality is delivering them a rotten egg sandwich when they ordered a vegan delight. Tim Urban, a popular Internet writer and author of the blog Wait But Why, takes it one step further by reducing happiness to a simple formula:

HAPPINESS = REALITY – EXPECTATIONS

Apparently this has been the millennial trap. Their expectations are too high or unrealistic, and as such they become disappointed in the real world, which leads to a degree of unhappiness or dissatisfaction. Urban refers to these millennials as GYPSY, "A GYPSY (Gen-Y Protagonists and Special Yuppies) is a unique brand of yuppie, one who thinks they are the main character of a very special story" (September, 2013).

Simon Sinek, author, motivational speaker and organisational consultant argues that one of the reasons for these unrealistic expectations is failed parenting strategies. Parents who coddled their children too much, told them how great or special they are, that they could have anything or achieve anything they wanted actually contributed to inflating their egos and sense of self, resulting in these high expectations.

There may be a bit of truth to this speculation, but isn't this just more unconstructive criticism, and the age-old strategy of blaming the parents? We all suffer from unmet expectations, which should lead us to believe that it's the expectations that need to be addressed.

When we have expectations, we are orchestrating the outcome in the way we behave, and what we say. When we have no expectations, anything is possible.

A quote by Sean Lyons, co-editor of *Managing the New Workforce: International Perspectives on the Millennial Generation* that really caught my attention:

"This generation has the highest likelihood of having unmet expectations with respect to their careers and the lowest levels of satisfaction with their careers at the stage that they're at. It is sort of a crisis of unmet expectations."

So what does this mean to you as a leader of millennials?

You find yourself in a situation where you are supervising millennials, maybe one, maybe several. You observe them, confident and self-assured, but somehow not quite team players, not taking initiative, and making outrageous demands. Or worse, not really saying anything. Perhaps you've never thought about what they need, you just want them to do their job. Or you've thought about how best to lead this young person, or team, but feel at a loss about how to motivate them.

First, however, we should understand what millennials expect from the workplace.

Studies show they want flexibility in their job, instant feedback and gratification for a job well done, a work/life balance, to be engaged in their work, someone who manages conflict, lots and lots of opportunities and an inspiring leader!

I can hear a few of you snickering; someone who motivates them and manages conflict. You are thinking, toughen up and manage your own conflict, motivate your own sorry self. The world isn't here to serve you. This is true. But millennials are being honest. We are asking what they need, and they are telling us. The question remains, do they have to adjust to the leadership styles of the past, or do we need to adapt to the millennials and the changing times in order to embrace their strengths. And, let's face it, they are the future and they do know some things that we don't.

They want to be inspired and to make an impact, and when that does not happen in the first few months of a new job, they become impatient and are quick to move on, as Maya was. According to the U.S. Bureau of Labor Statistics, members of this generation will have between six to seven jobs by the time they reach 26.

Ultimately, we may or may not agree with these millennial expectations but we certainly can't ignore them. They are going to be the biggest working population of the future. According to a Pew Research Center analysis of U.S. Census Bureau data, more than one in three American labour force participants (35 per cent) are millennials, making them the largest generation in the U.S. labour force.

The real question then is how do we work with them and lead them in a way that benefits them and the organisation? Instead of trying to come up with ways to reduce the expectations of millennials and make them more "realistic", why don't we try to find ways to meet them? At least the ones we have influence over. In his talk about millennials in 2016, Sinek commented:

> *"Corporate environments that are not helping them [the millennials] build their confidence. That aren't helping them learn the skills of cooperation. That aren't helping them overcome the challenges of a digital world and finding more balance. That isn't helping them overcome the need for instant gratification and teach them the joys and impact and the fulfilment you get from working hard on something for a long time that cannot be done in a month or even in a year.....*
> *They blame themselves. They think it's them who can't deal. And so it makes it all worse. It's not them. It's the corporations, it's the corporate environment, it's the total lack of good leadership in our world today that is making them feel the way they do. They were dealt a bad hand and it's the company's responsibility to pick up the slack and work extra hard and find ways to build their confidence, to teach them the social skills that they are missing out on."*

More often than not, millennials are finding themselves in corporate environments that are neither helping them nor encouraging good leadership. This has compounded their frustrations and increased their unmet expectations. The hard reality is that we need this workforce, we need them to stay on board, we need their skills and competencies, and we need to keep them engaged in the workplace. Companies therefore do have a responsibility to meet millennial expectations. By investing in millennials' growth and success, they would be investing in the growth and success of their company. A good leader, whom they can learn from and who inspires them in the workplace is already a step in the right direction.

And that, my friends, is a realistic expectation to meet.

#TheWorkplaceHasChanged

The workplace of today is unrecognisable compared to when baby boomers started their careers, in terms of the working environment, technology, demographics, cultural sensitivities, working remotely, and especially in how we lead.

In my first internship in 1998 at a multinational professional services company in Beirut, Lebanon, all our business communication took place over landlines, or in person, and all our documents were hard copies. The office layout was open plan except for the senior managers, who had their own offices. All staff had to be present in the office at all times, unless they were with clients. Lunch breaks were spent having a sandwich at your desk. That was the late '90s private sector, and in many ways it was already very advanced compared to other companies. Now, of course, the flexibility these companies give their employees is unparalleled. Remote office working, flexi-time - the location is not as important as output, and with these types of jobs, as long as you are reachable via email or phone, the job can always get done, regardless of where and when you do it.

Changing Mentality

I had a supervisor in the '90s who literally cut up reports I submitted and pasted them back together in a different order. I knew more about technology than she did, and she had no interest in learning. Some might say that these were the early days of what we now know as Cut and Paste. That supervisor had been part of the "cradle to grave" work mentality; having joined the institution at a young age, she had been there her whole career, and eventually she would retire from that same job. She was very much motivated by the Baby Boomer mentality of loyalty to an organisation and financial stability. Most of her communication was done over the telephone, she had a very high regard for authority and management, was competitive, and valued hard work, which was demonstrated by all the long hours on the job (but not necessarily increased output). She worked hard for a title and for promotions, status was significant, and she was always quick to correct people when they got her title wrong. She retired a few years later.

Times have changed. The "cradle to grave" concept has died.

As we know, the Baby Boomers have begun to retire. The oldest Boomers reached 65 in 2011, and the youngest will reach that milestone in 2029. That's another ten years that this group will be in the workforce, and likely longer as the retirement age in many companies is being raised to match increased life expectancy. So what we have are Boomers wanting to maintain their place in the workforce, likely as upper level management, and millennials trying to make an impact in the workforce. However, their needs seem to be more aligned than one would initially think. Boomers want to ease out of the workforce which means more flexibility, more remote working, and they do tend to be very tech-savvy (having developed skills over the last 15 years). Not surprisingly, millennials also want flexibility, remote working, and needless to say are tech-savvy.

Technology

Technology is a main driver in the workplace and has totally transformed the way we work. We can be connected anywhere, at any time, regardless of location. Businesses are global and people relocate around the world for jobs. Lynda Gratton, Professor of Management Practice at the London Business School (LBS) suggested that five billion people will be connected with mobile devices by 2025. The rise of smartphones, high-speed internet, online file sharing, and new software have changed the traditional working environment.

The modern workplace is all about social collaboration. We no longer need to be in the office to work and employees are given more accountability in delivering results, which does not depend on the time spent in the office, as long as the work gets done. There is much more fluidity in the workforce, with people going in and out at faster speeds, on project-based assignments. As a result, many companies now give their employees the flexibility to telecommute, to work from home and only to come into the office when necessary. You don't have to work at Google or Twitter to be part of these changes. In general, many companies have realised that to stay competitive and to attract millennials, they need to provide more flexibility for their employees. It's difficult to assess the percentage of professionals that work remotely. Google it and you will see studies that claim from 50-70 per cent depending on the industry and country, and the amount of flexibility that companies offer also varies. Some have philosophies that as long as the job gets done, it doesn't matter from where. Others offer one day a week, or occasional days. One thing that is for sure is that the numbers are rising.

The Work/Life Blend

Work used to be a place to go. Now it's something you do, sometimes wherever you feel like it. To many millennials, the notion of a 9-5 job seems... well, like a crazy concept that's not very efficient, because they experience life not as blocked-off periods of time but as something that flows, that is very interactive and flexible. Think of the huge transformation we have gone through in the last decades in terms of how we view our workspace. Previously, it was a desk, in an office, and you went there at 9 am and left at 5 pm. You took an hour for lunch, and when you went home, nobody from work contacted you. Now, you wake up, check your emails, respond to a few, make some phone calls on your way to work or from your kitchen table. Throughout the day you are able to engage in more than just work. When you feel like you need a break you could research your next vacation, or shop for a new bathroom cabinet. You can switch from work to leisure at the press of a button, and still be very efficient.

This work style is normal for millennials and leaders need to embrace it in order to satisfy them and prevent a feeling of being caged in.

Demographic Shift

More women have entered the workplace over the last ten years; consequently, diversity and gender inclusion are high on company agendas. Having more women in the workplace means that companies have had to come up with more initiatives to motivate and retain them. This is also in line with the rising trend of having a better work/life balance, allowing employees, especially working mothers, the flexibility to balance work demands with life responsibilities. Arianna Huffington, founder of The Huffington Post, once discussed the importance of having well-balanced employees that can make better and more effective decisions. This is why she created a "nap room" so that employees can take naps whenever they need to in order to "unplug and recharge", highlighting the importance of workplace flexibility and the significance of work/life balance.

Differing Employment Perspectives

With the millennials entering the workforce, perspectives regarding employment and jobs have shifted 180 degrees. Their perspective of success no longer depends on having a traditional career path. This generation is re-defining what success means in the workplace. A millennial can have differing degrees, ranging from business to the arts. Twenty years ago that CV would have been regarded as unfocused, but with this generation it shows curiosity, multi-talent, and passion.

There are endless articles about how millennials are quitters, leaving well-paying jobs to pursue their #bestlife, leaving poorly paid or uninspiring jobs in hopes of something more rewarding. Without personal gain or a motivation it seems obvious to them to move on. This takes us back to the notion that millennials seek a meaningful life. They are a generation that has easy access to whatever they desire – cheap travel, various means of communication, self-publishing, ideas and different ways of life, and the ability to roam, taste, try and experiment, with an audience of friends, followers and connections. So why stay in a job that provides little or none of that?

For the pay cheque of course, but apparently this doesn't have as much weight as we think. Millennials are all about start-ups, collaboration, and teamwork, but with them at the steering wheel.

Honestly, it's the companies that should be worried. Millennials make up an ever-increasing percentage of the workforce. Companies, and in particular HR professionals have had to adjust a lot of their ways of dealing with these new employment perspectives, in order to attract, motivate and retain the younger generations. Some companies even go the extra mile to help these employees in their career changes with initiatives such as learning and development classes, supportive internal transfer opportunities or rotational programmes. This is being done to grow employees' skill sets while providing them with the flexibility of making informed decisions and finding the perfect role for themselves. For example, nearly a quarter of DreamWorks' 2,200 employees are under the age of 30. They have adapted to the needs of the millennials by offering creative classes such as photography, sculpting, painting or karate that can be taken during office hours. Not surprising then that the company's retention rate is 96 per cent!

These changing workplace trends are moving in the right direction, very much in line with what millennials expect from the workplace. So why is it that millennials still face these disappointments and unmet expectations at work?

Hint: What do you have when high expectation meets inflexible leadership? The answer lies in the middle ground, the collaboration, and the acknowledgement that the world is changing... yep, still changing... hasn't stopped....

#LeadershipTypes

Up until recently, the notion of leadership was more defined. Leaders were the people who worked their way to the top of a vertically structured organisation. Essentially, they climbed the proverbial ladder - the focus wasn't so much on leading or mentoring as it was on a chain-of-command process. Decisions were made by upper level executives and passed on to middle management to implement. This type of structure often relied on strict protocols.

Today, however, companies are more often embracing what is known as a horizontal, or flat organisational structure. Employees are given more authority to make decisions without having to acquire executive approval. The focus is on empowering staff and creating an environment that is more creative, motivating, and fluid. By removing barriers between staff and executives, teamwork, collaboration and the exchange of ideas emerge organically.

A new style of leadership, based on trust, is all the rage. When shown trust and given a certain degree of autonomy, employees are easily able to formulate meaningful and productive working relationships. But when the trust has been breached, it's very difficult to rebuild. Research by the Harvard Business Review highlighted the manager-employee trust gap. Many employees say they feel their managers do not trust them. The result is that workplace productivity and engagement often suffer. Similarly, employees who are less trusted by their manager put forth less effort, are less productive, and are more likely to leave the organisation. So there is a ripple effect in both ways (HBR, 2017).

Leaders of today also need to be good at collaboration and influencing people, and they need to be skilled at trusting others, because they are more likely to use intrinsic rather than extrinsic motivations with others. They will need to operate from a clear set of values and principles, because opportunistic or selfish motives would be seen and rejected, and above all, they are not dependent on direct authority or political power (Forbes, 2012). With the right traits and characteristics, anyone can be a leader, which brings us back to Sharma and the concept of a leader who doesn't need a title.

What is the transformational style of leadership?

This style embraces change and achieves positive outcomes. It consists of four elements:

IDEALISED INFLUENCE: the degree to which the leader instils values, beliefs, respect, a strong sense of purpose, and a collective sense of mission

INTELLECTUAL STIMULATION: the ability to accept different perspectives and stimulate thinking

INDIVIDUALISED CONSIDERATION: appreciating each individual's contribution

INSPIRATIONAL MOTIVATION: the ability to motivate and inspire subordinates

This style of leadership is based on encouraging and promoting followers to align with organisational goals to attain performance objectives.

If you google "traits of successful leaders", the results will show everything from integrity, high emotional intelligence, self-awareness, authenticity, ability to motivate and inspire employees, good communication, commitment, passion, honesty, being innovative and a creative thinker. The list goes on and on. So how do we know what to home in on when leading millennials?

Deloitte's 2018 Human Capital survey proposes that the 21st century career model will mainly focus on continuous reskilling and gaining new experiences. There will also be a growing requirement for complex problem-solving (63 per cent), cognitive abilities (55 per cent), and cultural/social skills (52 per cent). Millennials are the workforce of the 21st century, so following an old-school approach to leadership just doesn't cut it. As a leader it's your responsibility to stay on top of current trends and concerns in the workplace, to know what motivates your team, and above all, to not hold them back because of preconceived notions of power.

The vertical structure in many organisations won't decompose overnight, and as a result, the millennials may find themselves jostled around as this antiquated structure based on outdated beliefs attempts to update (think of a sluggish computer operating system trying to update software).

Many companies send their mid-to-senior-management to leadership trainings in an attempt to shrink the gap between old and new leadership styles. Often one of the pre-course reading materials is "Leadership that Gets Results", an article by psychologist, author and science journalist Daniel Goleman, first published in the Harvard Business Review (HBR, 2000). Goleman discusses the different leadership styles and specifically refers to six encountered in the workplace. They are explained as follows:

COERCIVE LEADER:

The "do what I say" approach, top-down decision-making which may be effective in times of crisis but for the most part tends to reduce employee motivation and flexibility

AUTHORITATIVE LEADER:

The "come with me" approach, stating the overall goal but giving employees the freedom to choose their own ways of achieving it. The leader tends to have a vision and motivates people towards that vision. According to Goleman, it is one of the most effective leadership styles, however it may not work fully if that leader is working with a team of experts who are more technically knowledgeable than he/she is, as they may regard him/her as out of touch

AFFILIATIVE LEADER:

The "people come first" attitude, which encourages teamwork and increases morale. This approach primarily revolves around keeping people happy, it's a very collaborative form of leadership; but the leader offers no advice and poor performance is not addressed properly

DEMOCRATIC LEADER:

Gives voice to the employees in decision-making, these leaders build organisational flexibility and responsibility and help generate fresh ideas, but too much involvement can also lead to confusion and employees feeling leaderless, especially in times of crisis

PACESETTING LEADER:

An approach that sets high performance standards. The style creates high motivation levels with employees who are self-motivated, however this type of leader's demand for excellence can be overwhelming

COACHING:

Focused more on personal development, it improves work performance because there is a lot of emphasis on continuous dialogue, however this type of leadership is not effective when employees are in an environment that is resistant to change and personal development

On the one hand, this article is useful because it provides a good overview of different types of leadership while discussing the pros and cons of each, and highlighting which climate they should be used in.

On the other hand, it was written 19 years ago, and much has changed in the workplace. It doesn't address how technology and remote and flexible working have changed this environment. Leaders need to be more adaptable and insightful than ever before.

What to do with this information? Be **aware** that different leadership models exist. **Understand** why each of them works or doesn't in your workplace. **Adapt** accordingly to lead your people.

Although you as an individual don't have the power (or perhaps you do!) to change an organisation's structure, the more awareness and understanding you have on how to motivate and inspire the millennials, the more successful you will be.

For example, if you are overseeing a team in a vertically structured bank, you may not have the freedom to let them operate in a horizontal way, but you can still offer them trust, and a degree of autonomy. Create an environment within the team that mimics what you value. This approach can be contagious, with team members instinctively following suit. Remember that daily interactions count just as much as the company philosophy.

PART II

THE SURVEY

In total, over 700 respondents completed the online survey; about a third of the data collected was from attendees at the 2018 One Young World Summit and the rest through my immediate professional network, extended network, and social media channels. The information obtained provides the foundation for this book. My goal was to give millennials like Maya a voice and try to better understand what makes them tick, what motivates them, what they desire in the workplace, and discover, what are the traits of their ideal leader.

What is One Young World?

According to their website:

"At the heart of every global threat is a failure of leadership. This new generation is the most informed, most educated, most connected generation in human history. One Young World identifies, promotes and connects the world's most impactful young leaders to create a better world, with more responsible, more effective leadership.

The annual One Young World Summit convenes the brightest young talent from every country and sector, working to accelerate social impact. Delegates from 190+ countries are counselled by influential political, business and humanitarian leaders such as Justin Trudeau, Paul Polman and Meghan Markle, amongst many other global figures.

Delegates participate in four transformative days of speeches, panels, networking and workshops. All Delegates have the opportunity to apply to give keynote speeches, sharing a platform with world leaders with the world's media in attendance. The agenda is shaped by the One Young World Community through the Global Consultation Process, ensuring maximum relevance to the issues affecting young people. As well as listening to keynote speakers, Delegates have the opportunity to challenge, interact and be mentored by world leaders."

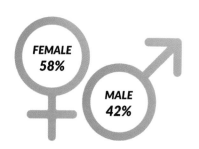

FEMALE 58%

MALE 42%

19-26 YEARS OLD **35%**

27-34 YEARS OLD **65%**

EDUCATION

High School Diploma	11%
Some college, but no degree	11%
Undergraduate Bachelor's Degree	37%
Postgraduate Master's Degree	37%
Doctorate Degree	4%

WHERE DO YOU WORK?

Africa	11%
Asia	10%
Australia & New Zealand	1%
Europe	33%
Latin America & the Caribbean	4%
MENA (Middle East & North Africa)	11%
North America & Canada	30%

WHAT IS YOUR NATIONALITY?

Africa	14%
Asia	13%
Australia & New Zealand	1%
Europe	30%
Latin America & the Caribbean	7%
MENA (Middle East & North Africa)	11%
North America & Canada	24%

WHAT IS YOUR CURRENT JOB LEVEL?

Owner / Executive / C-Level	9%
Senior Management	8%
Middle Management	23%
Intermediate	28%
Entry Level	23%
Other	9%

WHAT SECTOR DO YOU WORK IN?

Sector	Percentage
Public	28%
Private	44%
Academia	7%
NGO / Civil Service	12%
Other	9%

HOW MUCH WORK EXPERIENCE DO YOU HAVE?

Experience	Percentage
Less than 1 year	13%
1 – 3 Years	21%
3 – 5 Years	20%
5 Years & above	46%

One of the survey questions asked respondents:

Upon joining the workplace, did you have expectations regarding the following aspects that were not met?

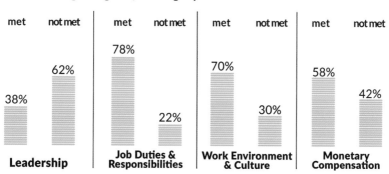

	met	not met
Leadership	38%	62%
Job Duties & Responsibilities	78%	22%
Work Environment & Culture	70%	30%
Monetary Compensation	58%	42%

Remember at the beginning of the book when we talked about the millennial trap; expectations vs. reality which more often than not leads to unfulfilled expectations and unhappiness in the workplace? Our survey results highlighted a similar outcome.

Based on four main factors in the workplace:

LEADERSHIP

JOB DUTIES & RESPONSIBILITIES

WORK ENVIRONMENT & CULTURE

MONETARY COMPENSATION

62 per cent of the survey respondents said that their leaders **were not** meeting their expectations.

42 per cent of the survey respondents felt their compensation expectations **were not** being met; or in other words, the pay was shit! Although money is not typically a primary factor for millennials in the workplace, this question is focused on millennial expectations when they first entered the workplace.

The results for Job Duties & Responsibilities and Work Environment & Culture are more positive because 78 per cent and 70 per cent of respondents highlighted that their expectations **were met** in these aspects.

This means that even if millennials are not inspired by the actions, behaviours and traits of their supervisors, they are in fact working on assignments that they enjoy, or that motivate, engage and fulfil them; and doing this in a positive environment where they feel comfortable, in a culture that promotes collaboration and a sense of purpose.

#WhatTheySaid

During the time I was writing this book I became hyperaware of how people comment on millennials. It wasn't just the harshness with which they judged them, but the frequency. Somehow millennials have become a target, easy to dismiss as "entitled", easy to generalise as "lazy", and easy to label "screen addicts". I also developed much more compassion towards this group, who have to defend themselves on a daily basis just for being born into the information age, for having Baby Boomer parents, for being passionate as opposed to compliant, and for realising early on that living #mybestlife is not about being selfish, it's about living!

Yes, they love their avocado on toast and matcha lattes and we love to mock this and ask what's wrong with jam on toast, and regular coffee. Well, regular coffee is what their grandparents drink, and jam is screaming sugar. But besides that, nothing wrong with doing things the way we have always done them...But should we really want to do things the way we have always done them? Should we not be aiming for change and progress?

Do millennials think about their future, their contribution, their legacy, or are they really just living in the moment being their selfish little avocado-eating selves, snapping selfies to preserve the moment?

Judging from their answers, they have goals, values, are passionate about causes, and expect the best from life because hey, there is no rewind button on life, only refresh!

One of the questions asked the respondents:

If you were retiring today, what is the legacy you would want to leave behind in the workplace?

And here are some of the things they said:

"As someone who was fair and who treated everyone with respect"

"I want to be remembered as someone who helped humanity"

"As someone who brought happiness to people"

"As someone who built the organisation from scratch to an institution that is positively impacting on the lives of thousands of people"

"That I did everything with heart"

"That I created opportunities for people"

"That I mentored and raised up a new generation of leaders"

"As someone who did everything with passion and for passion"

"That I created a skilled and engaged team, who are self-motivated to continue to do bigger and better things in my absence"

"That I inspired, even if it's just one person, to do better"

"As a person who values other people's opinions and was able to listen and to mentor"

I was recently invited to a job interview for the position of Head of the Human Resources Function for a mid-sized NGO. The interview panel consisted of six people; three who would be part of my team and the other three part of Management. However, what surprised me (pleasantly so) is that the junior staff, all in their 20s, i.e. millennials, were not only invited to attend the interview but also allowed to ask questions. And they asked really tough questions. They dug right into my management experience, asked about challenges I have had working in teams, how I resolved problems, and my leadership style. The questions were behavioural-based, serious and very direct. These questions were coming from my potential direct reports. This made me want to work for this NGO even more, because it showed that they were taking their young staff members seriously and were giving them an opportunity to be involved in the decision-making process of who would eventually be recruited as their boss. I found this level of employee engagement impressive. As the interview was coming to an end, and I was asked whether I had any questions for them, I decided to drop my pre-rehearsed questions regarding job role, responsibilities, compensation, and instead asked my three (potential) colleagues this: In one word, can you tell me what is the most important thing you are looking for in your leader? They were a bit taken aback by the direct question, but composed themselves very quickly.

The responses:

EMOTIONAL INTELLIGENCE
EXCELLENT COMMUNICATION
PROBLEM-SOLVER

There it was straight from the source: three traits that were highly valued. This interview was one of the most interesting ones I had ever been to. It gave me a good insight regarding what millennials want in their leader and provided a lot of food for thought as to whether I even possessed these traits. It caused me to self-reflect on my strengths and weaknesses as a potential leader, which rarely happens after an interview. Involving them in the interview panel had been a win-win solution. This goes to show that interviews can be a two-way street. Both the organisation and the candidate need to assess whether they are the right fit for each other. For me, it was an opportunity to meet the types of people I would be working with and get a glimpse at the company culture, which seemed friendly, open, transparent and informal (to the point where the management and staff were laughing and joking with each other before the interview started). For them, it was a chance to understand what they would be getting if I was hired and what kind of a leader I would be.

The survey results showed something very similar. The second part of the online survey listed 25 characteristics that respondents were asked to rank on a scale from 1 (most agreeable) to 5 (least agreeable) in terms of what they considered to be important leadership qualities. There were nine traits that ranked the highest.

And basically, what Millennials want is a
CHAMELEON.

THE CHAMELEON LEADER

The percentages refer to the number of survey participants who rated this trait as very important

79%	56%	63%	59%	51%	60%	54%	54%	50%
C	**H**	**A**	**M**	**E**	**L**	**E**	**O**	**N**

Communicate
Honesty
Accountability
Motivate
Emotional Intelligence
Listen
Ethical
Overcome Obstacles
Nodal

So a CHAMELEON LEADER means...

The most unique characteristic of the chameleon is its ability to change colour, to adapt and blend in to any surroundings. Some chameleons can change colour to hide themselves, others change colours based on how they're feeling. Chameleons can rapidly adapt to new circumstances and are very much in tune with their internal and external environments. In the current rapidly changing work environment, flexibility and adaptability are key leadership qualities.

A popular observation based on the ideas of Charles Darwin:

> **"It's not the biggest, the brightest, or the best that will survive, but those who adapt the quickest."**

As the chameleon, by nature, is hard to spot, this suggests an invisible type of leadership; one that is guiding, advising and coaching employees but not necessarily always from the front line; a leader who can influence and who leads without leading in the conventional sense; kind of like the leader with no title.

Equally distinctive are the chameleon's eyes which rotate and focus independently, which means they can observe two different objects simultaneously. This enables the chameleon to properly survey its surroundings and pay close attention to what is happening around them. Being able to read situations, gain the full picture before making judgments and just being in observation mode and listening are important characteristics for any leader. The chameleon also has a 360-degree angle allowing them to scan their environment and have a holistic, "helicopter view", looking beyond what's right in front of them to view the bigger perspective.

Lastly, the chameleon is humble by nature and comfortable in his own skin (until he sheds it). As a leader, the chameleon may not be at the head of the pack, nor shout out their qualities to everyone in sight, but they will blend into the environment, lead from the sidelines and still effect the necessary change. This kind of leader demonstrates confidence and modesty, and their decisions are based on the collaborative input of their employees and situations rather than ego and fanfare.

As depicted by Lao Tzu in the *Tao Te Ching*:

"The best leaders are those the people hardly know exist. The next best is a leader who is loved and praised.

Next comes the one who is feared.
The worst one is the leader that is despised."

#TalkLikeAMillennial

One of the questions asked the respondents:

If you could put a huge billboard in the workplace with ONE message on it, i.e. your motto, a quote or your favourite saying, what would it be?

"Nothing happens in the comfort zone"

"I don't know is always a valid answer"

"What would you do if you weren't afraid?"

"Don't act like a leader. BE a leader"

"Imagination is more important than knowledge. Knowledge is limited. Imagination encircles the world"

"Never stop learning"

"Inspire and be inspired"

"Life belongs to those who show up"

"It's ok to fail. Just pick yourself back up, learn from it and keep going"

"You can only grow if you let others grow too"

"Evolve every day"

"We are what we repeatedly do"

"Happiness is a choice"

"Leave your ego outside"

"Earn Your pay cheque"

What advice would you give to younger generations entering the workplace? Any words of wisdom?

"Don't let anyone look down on you because you are young"

"Accept that there is constant change, nothing is fixed"

"Be a source of motivation to those around you through your words and deeds"

"Don't let them tell you that you're too young or not right for a certain job. Work hard and prove your worth"

"Manage your expectations and just focus on doing a good job. Nothing ever really turns out exactly the way we want it to"

"Master your craft"

"Forget this idea of a conventional career - make your own path"

"Don't be demotivated from the start. Be patient. Your time will come"

"Expect the unexpected. Being able to adapt is key"

"It's not about the job. It's about a good leader. They are the biggest factor in your career success"

"If you aren't exactly sure what you are doing and what path you want to take, it's okay. Most people are still trying to figure it out at this stage"

"Inspire those below you, around you, above you. Leadership has no title"

"Don't worry about failing. It's a sign of strength, not weakness"

"Learn as much as you can from a good leader"

PART III

THE CHAMELEON LEADER

#ChooseToLead

Leaders begin at the fork in the road. You have the choice to either wave your employee/team absently down a path with no option but to find their way, or you can choose to accompany them and create a collaborative, inspiring journey. The conscious leaders, the ones who choose to be aware of what constitutes a good leader, come equipped, prepared to not only guide, but also to follow. As stated in the Harvard Business Review, August 2018:

"To be a good leader, start by being a good follower."

This is one of my favourite stories from a survey respondent because it truly shows that millennials want to be heard, can add value, have skills, and yet can so easily be crushed by a leader who doesn't choose to lead.

Anthony has been working with a communications firm for almost two years. This is his second job since graduating from a Communications programme. For the most part he is content in his workplace, but he doesn't really feel his supervisor values his feedback. Recently, he was working on a project and realised that they weren't reaching their target audience in the best possible way. He went to his supervisor and suggested they try a different approach, and made a suggestion. His boss responded by saying, "I've been doing this a lot longer than you, trust me."

Anthony's thought, although he kept it to himself, was: but I know a lot more about this than you. Social media is something I do every day, not something my kid showed me how to use.

Anthony, 27,
social media manager at a marketing
agency in Amsterdam, The Netherlands

Apparently you will have better influence as a leader if you are perceived as one of the group you are leading, as opposed to one who distances themselves for the sake of respect. In a recent article published in the British Journal of Psychology (May 2018) the author talks about the 'we' and the 'I' approach. If you position yourself as part of the collective 'we', then you gain more respect from your team than if you position yourself above them.

Just because you are the supervisor or leader of your team doesn't mean you don't still have something to learn. Millennials get such a bad rap from the media that we tend to dismiss them without hearing them out. The truth is they do know things, especially about social media and technology that we may be aware of, but don't necessarily know as intimately. Their perspective can add a lot of value to a team, so take a moment and listen, and don't hesitate to follow once in a while.

For me, a leader is someone who I can learn from and who challenges me to be at my best. I have been working for the past ten years, and I find it so disappointing that in this time only one person has allowed me to reach my full potential. Perhaps this is because I've chosen to work in the public sector, which is notorious for its bureaucracy and inefficiency, but it's been disappointing nonetheless. This is not to say that my working life has been full of complete failures in leadership (well, perhaps only one) but that only one in my opinion had all the traits of an ideal leader.

As a so-called "millennial" working amongst older colleagues, I do feel the generational gap most of the time. Perhaps this is a result of their time and treatment as young professionals, but many of my older colleagues give you the feeling that you need to earn your place amongst them, often belittling my own talents or abilities and ignoring any experience or skills I do possess. And as an 'elder millennial' I wonder how much longer I will be perceived as a young professional. I feel that this work culture is changing (in some places more than others) and I hope that the next generation entering the workforce does not experience the same.

Fatma, 30,
communications officer at an international
development institution in Vienna, Austria

Since you have picked up this book, already interested in becoming a better leader for the millennials, have continued to read and found yourself curious about these nine traits that define the CHAMELEON Leader, then let's get on with it and take an in-depth look at what millennials have declared to be desirable in their fearless leaders.

#Communicate

"It is NOT my way or the highway."

Survey respondent

Communication is the ability to get your ideas into the minds of others. Speaking, writing, and body language are all powerful ways to communicate and the key with millennials is to drop the authoritative tone and speak with the assumption that you are on a level playing field.

Understanding what is going on, what is expected of them, and feeling in the information loop is what keeps this group engaged. Good communication is an important skill for creating relationship networks, influencing and inspiring people, and collaborating effectively.

One of the survey questions posed to millennials was: How would you prefer your supervisor communicates with you (1 = most preferred / 4 = least preferred). The results showed that in the workplace, ***in-person communication was still the preferred option*** (with a score of 3.32), followed by email (2.52), phone (2.45) and finally video-conferencing (1.71).

This outcome is surprising and contradicts the many articles written about millennials in the workplace. The notion that just because millennials live and breathe technology, they prefer it as the main tool of communication in the workplace, is not entirely true. Are millennials going back to the basics (at least in the workplace)? A survey of 40,000 people worldwide conducted between the Center for Effective Organizations at the USC Marshall School of Business and London Business School in association with Pricewaterhouse-Coopers showed that while in their private lives, millennials are more likely to use technology than Gen X; for example, instant messaging (39 per cent and 24 per cent), texting (59 per cent and 39 per cent) and social networks (67 per cent and 49 per cent), at work, they are more "old school". Surprised? That makes two of us! The study went on to highlight that millennials overwhelmingly chose face-to-face meetings as their top choice (80 per cent). These results even extended to communication with their supervisors regarding performance evaluations, career planning and compensation.

"When I meet with my supervisor in person, I get clearer guidance on what is expected of me, and it's a more efficient way of communicating than emailing each other all day long and not making any real progress."

David, 27

So, yes they are tech-savvy, and yes, they may be glued to their phones in their personal lives, but at work, the HOW of communicating with millennials in the workplace is to ditch the phones, limit emails to less urgent items, and up the face-to-face communication.

- *79 per cent of millennials rated communication as the most important trait in a leader*

- *When communicating, speak their language, which is informal, provide them with the whole context of projects, what is expected of them, and perceived outcomes, preferably in face-to-face meetings. However, don't be afraid to use the screen to provide bite-sized bits of information to keep them up to date and in the loop.*

- *Make content engaging – use visuals, infographics, photos and videos (sorry to say, but PowerPoint is old-school for these guys). Consider self-directed training (as opposed to long generalised workshops) that takes into consideration different learning styles and paces.*

The following story came from a sit-down meeting with one of the survey respondents. It truly highlights how top-down leadership and poor, disrespectful communication can have a huge impact on a millennial's career and motivation.

I was surprised by the harsh communication between doctors and the different levels in the hospital, i.e. nurses, doctors, and heads of specialised departments. Maybe it's because they are carrying a lot of responsibility or stress, but either way the basics of communication were missing. During my three-year residency, I was working under one doctor who was my senior, and as per the usual practice, all my communication about patient analysis and problems had to go through him. I would call him to tell him the details of a patient and to check on the next steps, and he would be shouting at me on the phone, "I don't care about the details, just tell me what she has now". Very rough, direct, rude, lacking any kind of compassion. It was demotivating. I was frustrated and angry most of the time. Above all, how he spoke to me and others was to talk down at us, and to shout. I know we were still juniors but I was there to learn, and this kind of environment that he created was not conducive to learning. On various occasions, I thought about quitting the programme but I had worked so hard to get in that I didn't want to give up because of that one supervisor. After a while though, I did ask to be transferred to a different department, even though it was not the specialisation I wanted, but it was the only way to not work with this particular doctor. I realised that a supervisor can make or break your career, and can impact how much you like or don't like your job. It's already been five years since I finished my residency and I am working in a hospital with millennials that now report to me, and I always make an effort to treat them with respect, fairness and to provide mentorship when I can. Talking to them (or anyone, really) in a disrespectful manner makes no sense because not only does it affect this person negatively but if you don't communicate right, then it also creates a culture of fear where they cannot come to tell you if they have made a mistake, and in a hospital the consequences of this can be fatal. If they tell you what they did wrong at the beginning, then I can help them take responsibility, potentially mend the situation and they can learn from it. Otherwise, it's just a slippery slope downwards.

Philip, 33,
medical doctor at a private hospital
in Vienna, Austria

#Honesty

"Leadership is about positively influencing the lives of those around you, which can be achieved with honesty and authenticity."

Survey respondent

Directness, honesty, and transparency are traits that millennials value. Perhaps this is the result of growing up online where there is no place to hide, and with an altered sense of privacy, but if there is anything millennials feel entitled to, it's information and being in-the-know. For example, if you are aware that changes are going to happen to a project that your team members are working on, tell them. If you know that one of your staff members is not going to receive a promotion that he/she is waiting for, tell them. If you did not like the report that was prepared for you, tell them. More often than not, millennials feel discouraged in the workplace because they feel that their leaders are not being open and honest with them, which then creates an emotional distance.

"My supervisor is not able to have an open and honest conversation especially when it comes to difficult situations. So the issue is usually ignored and ignored until it becomes much worse. It would be better for morale and in general for work productivity if he would just be straight with me and tell me what's on his mind and what the problem is instead of dancing around it."

Erika, 26

The main area flagged by millennials as greatly affecting a sense of honesty was being authentic. A lot of respondents said they wanted leaders that were "real". The question is, what does "real" mean to someone who grew up heavily under the influence of "virtual"? I found this to be an interesting concept because in my mind, a lot of the things that millennials are heavily invested in are "unreal". Social media platforms thrive on the manipulation of reality. The aim is to get followers and likes, regardless of the authenticity of the image.

For anyone who watches the British science-fiction series, *Black Mirror*, specifically season 3, episode 1, "Nosedive", we see the virtual world taken to a new level - where people rate each other with stars (5 is the maximum) for every interaction they have. The impact on their living and socioeconomic standing is remarkable, taking the notion of social media to a different level.

However, when it comes to the real world workplace, millennials surprise us again. They claim to want authenticity.

Authenticity in leadership means having no shame in admitting weakness or failures. When millennials feel their leaders are just as human as they are, they feel an emotional connection. In the 2005 commencement address at Stanford University, Steve Jobs said, "Truth be told, this is the closest I've ever gotten to a college graduation", and proceeded to explain why he dropped out of college. Some of the students said they had expected him to talk about his successes, not his failures. That's the hallmark of an authentic leader. They are not afraid to talk about their failures. So the lesson learned: presenting the perfect façade is OUT for this generation; it's not seen as a sign of strength but rather weakness. And showing your weaknesses is a sign of strength!

> **"Vulnerability is the birthplace of innovation,
> creativity and change."**
> *Brené Brown*

One thing I consider that a leader should do is to be inclusive of everyone's opinion and give each person the opportunity to think creatively and just to be honest about what we are doing right or wrong.

My previous boss, who luckily did not last long in his position, lacked any kind of leadership skills and my work and morale (as well as that of my co-workers) suffered as a result. Firstly, he did not possess any kind of vision for the work that we do, which left us without a purpose and stuck in an endless cycle of routine tasks. Even upon bringing in new ideas, he would not take the time to properly understand, or highjack the idea and execute it as his own, which alienated a lot of us. Moreover, he did not take the time to understand the work we were doing and instead decided to work in silos (a favourite word of his). Within months of him taking the position, we no longer worked as a team, as he stopped our regular meetings and did not take the time to ensure that we were in the loop of what was going on. As a result of his mismanagement, our workloads became uneven and our motivation plummeted.

Right now I have a leader who inspires me as well as others on my team. She has taken the time and possesses the emotional intelligence of someone who recognises our strengths and weaknesses and empowers us to develop our strengths and encourages us to work on our weaknesses. In her feedback she has been honest with me about my weaknesses, which, although I don't like to hear, I appreciate precisely because the feedback is constructive. Moreover, she understands the value of teamwork and practises this in our work, even when it comes to her asking us for help when she is in need. I feel safe giving my feedback and presenting my work as I know that my ideas will be encouraged and not ignored and because I have been given the opportunity to work autonomously and independently.

Frida, 28,
communications specialist at a Public Relations agency
in London, United Kingdom

#Accountability

> *"Allow for errors. Build a culture of taking risks, changing the status quo and staying accountable for your actions."*
>
> Survey respondent

Accountability was rated as the second most important trait by millennials. Millennials want their leaders to take responsibility for their choices, behaviours, and actions!

Take a moment to reflect on your leadership performance.

- *Are you honest and upfront when it comes to sharing information with your team and clients?*

- *Are you presenting your most authentic self, or in other words not operating under false pretences, or trying to appear a certain way?*

- *Are your motives genuine?*

- *Do you throw others under the bus in order to save face? Do you let your team members take the blame for things that were your responsibility?*

One of the survey respondents, Paul, 29, works in an international finance company where there is a lot of pressure from board members. The organisational structure is very top-down and Paul's boss often assigns him work that falls under the boss's responsibility. Paul confessed that there was a particular situation where he was to give a presentation to board members, using information and data given by his boss. Turns out the data wasn't accurate and the board members started asking difficult questions. His boss was in the meeting but didn't say a word in Paul's defence. Paul was very angry but didn't say anything to his boss and says he doesn't trust him and will likely start looking for another position soon.

This is a very common situation faced in the workplace and one that can be easily avoided if leaders acknowledge, "With power comes responsibility". More and more we seem to be living in a blame culture where individuals and organisations too easily pass the buck instead of showing some integrity and owning their messes.

Transparency is a popular term used in the workplace these days, meaning essentially that information be made accessible and willingly presented to team members, staff, and in some cases clients, in order to create an environment that feels open and trustworthy. People like to know what is going on, whether it be the steps of a project, the outcome of a decision, or simply an exchange of ideas. Millennials are particularly sensitive to being in the information loop because to them, children of the "information age", information is power. This generation does not operate in a bubble, quite the opposite - privacy is not something, for the most part, they feel entitled to, or even think about. To some, it may even imply being secretive, or having something to hide.

Millennials learn accountability from their leaders. They want to feel pride in the people they work with. When you as a leader model "accountable behaviour", when you deliver on promises and take responsibility for your actions, this encourages positive behaviour in millennials. This is top-down, lead by example, which naturally contributes to the company culture. When millennials work with leaders that follow poor accountability standards, then we have a big problem, because the circle of inefficiency goes round and round with no end. If there are no consequences, then it sends a message to everyone in the organisation that a lack of accountability is acceptable, which encourages mediocrity and does not contribute to a positive work environment. As a leader, when you fall short, correct it and get back on course. As Winston Churchill said:

"The price of greatness is responsibility."

This accountability link goes both ways. Not only do millennials want it from their leaders, but they also want their leader to hold them accountable for their performance. Gallup (2016) found that millennials crave accountability. Their study discovered that the engagement for millennials is 29 per cent, however, when their leaders held them accountable at work, this figure rose to 56 per cent.

My supervisor, head of project management, is so inspiring. She motivates me to take full responsibility. She trusts me, while guiding and helping me to be fully accountable for my clients and gives me the freedom I need. As long as the job gets done, she allows me to run the accounts in whatever way I choose. She doesn't mind if I start work late or early in the day in order to finish at a certain time or get a yoga session in. At the moment I am working harder than I ever have but I very much enjoy working for her and love the job. It doesn't feel like hard work because I am thriving on the challenge. My work is a reflection of myself and I get a lot of recognition for what I do. The freedom I am receiving in return for my hard work makes me want to work even harder.

Jill, 28,
project manager, Natives (student specialist marketing group)
in Brighton, United Kingdom

Guide for being more accountable:

- **Set clear goals and objectives of what is to be achieved (as stated before, don't communicate this in an excruciatingly boring and long-winded presentation; but rather, short, direct and visually is your best bet)**

- **Define the roles, responsibilities and accountability criteria for each member**

- **Be clear about the deadlines**

- **Clarify how this project/assignment contributes to the overall goals of the organisation**

- **Conduct regular follow-up on the status of the project; empower but don't micro-manage. Cheer them on if they are on track to meet deadlines and allow them to come up with alternative solutions if they are not**

- **Be present and show support if there are any questions along the way. Play the role of a mentor and coach; talk with them, not at them. Remember, this is a bottoms-up approach so no bossy, condescending behaviour. Opt for a participatory, collaborative approach. The aim is to get mutual commitment to action**

- *Allow them to feel ownership and hold them accountable for completing their part in that project*

- *Take personal responsibility for your part in any conversation. If you misunderstand something or make a mistake, admit it*

- *Communicate ahead of time what the next steps are or the consequences if the deadline is not met*

- *Demonstrate immediate accountability by either celebrating or confronting results*

None of these points are rocket science, more like common sense. Whenever you feel the urge to blame your co-worker, shred a file, or dodge a meeting and let the closest millennial cover for you, think again!

#Motivate

"Your actions should inspire others to dream more"
Survey respondent

One of the survey questions asked millennials, is your current leader someone who motivates you? The results showed that 56 per cent of respondents said *Yes*; the good news is that more than half of the respondents are motivated by their supervisors; the bad news is that almost half are not.

Motivation is a tricky thing, and much discussed among psychologists, coaches, leaders, and even parents. The question is, can you motivate someone else? At its most basic level, motivation provides someone with a reason for doing something. Naturally it ranked high among traits required by millennials of their leaders. For millennials to stay in their jobs (remember how they are always accused of being flighty and lacking company loyalty), they need to feel motivated! This motivation can stem from the company's goals and missions, a social purpose that the company is part of or a positive, collaborative work environment. But most importantly, motivation needs to come from strong leadership.

Motivating a team or an individual is no easy feat. How do you get someone to engage, to be effective, to be productive, and inspired? The key to motivating millennials (based on what they have told me) is to help them to be successful. This boils down to two factors: Mentoring and Opportunities (MO). These need to become the "modus operandi" or "method of operation" in the workplace when discussing motivation in relation to the millennials. For leaders, this should become a habit or rather a "way of operating", not an ad hoc exercise.

Let's take a closer look at their MO...

Mentoring: Millennials respond positively to collaboration, participation and mutual dialogue. Mentoring is particularly important as millennials have a desire for relationships of mutual respect, which is very much intertwined with the way they are communicated with and listened to. A good mentor will be involved in their career path, both in their current roles and beyond, guiding and advising them when needed; providing regular feedback on their performance or how to improve; someone who genuinely cares about their well-being, and who inspires them along the way. If millennials feel that they can trust their leader, and that this person is helping them on their path to success, their loyalty, commitment and productivity will be boundless.

According to the 2016 Deloitte Millennial Survey, younger professionals intending to stay with their organisation for more than five years are twice as likely to have a mentor as not (68 per cent to 32 per cent, respectively). It is therefore not only crucial for developing skills but also for retaining staff. In doing so, it is important to treat them like peers; you are not lecturing them, you are not talking down to them, you are conversing with them.

> *"I wish my supervisor would understand that there isn't such a defined line between our work and personal lives. I like to check and reply to emails when I have a free few minutes – maybe this is at midnight, or the weekend, but I also like to be able to shop online for a few minutes at work, or post something on Instagram. It's a flow, when I think of something I do it, and everything gets done!"*
>
> Lucy, 25

Some years ago in my previous place of employment, I attended a mandatory company-wide town hall meeting, where we had to listen to speech after speech on the performance of the company. At one point I noticed I had 30 WhatsApp messages (in a time span of four minutes). As I hurriedly unlocked my phone dreading some family emergency, I noticed that all messages were coming from one group, a group that had been created exactly four minutes ago, labelled "OH MY GOD" with a profile picture of Janice, Chandler Bing's annoying on-and-off girlfriend in the popular '90s sitcom *Friends*. This group had three members, myself and two millennial staff who had been hired as young professionals and who were my mentees. As I scrolled down, there was picture after picture of hilarious GIFs, memes and emojis, to highlight the level of boredom we had reached in that meeting. There were no full sentences or even words, yet we understood each other perfectly by the visuals that were circulating. My point is, the mentorship dynamic is very effective with millennials. We can joke and laugh about trivial things, and the next day we will have a serious dialogue about performance. This cultivates a long-term working relationship based on trust and understanding, which is priceless.

Opportunities: For millennials, learning and growth opportunities are key to keeping them engaged. Professional development and training has to be emphasised at all times. They are a big motivator for this generation.

> **"When I joined the organisation I was surprised by the lack of intellectual engagement, since the day-to-day tasks don't require a high level of thinking. I was craving something I could get excited about."**
>
> *Ana, 25*

This is a comment made by a 25-year-old who has been in the workplace for less than two years. Millennials need a learning curve, and to keep them motivated, it is the responsibility of leaders to provide it because despite what many think, millennials are serious about investing in their careers. For them opportunities to learn, develop new skill sets and grow into leaders is the real prize.

As a leader you need to be serious about helping them build their skills in a way that is consistent with their career ambitions and at the same time will create a talent pipeline for the organisation. What does that mean in practical terms?

Create a learning environment: One way to do this is by providing opportunities to learn on the job and online training.

> **"In the food processing company I work for, every now and then, our management encourages team members to work on projects that may not be part of their job role, and they love it, because it gives them an opportunity to get creative and learn more about other areas of the business."**
>
> *Carol, 30*

A Gallup Report (2016) showed that learning on the job is important to the majority of millennials (87 per cent). They want to learn from peers and co-workers just as much as they want to learn from industry experts. Employers that create and deliver courses online are well matched with the millennials' appetite for training because it enables them to access the training at the moment they need it from any of their devices. This allows them flexibility in both time and location. As digital natives, the millennials are less interested in formal classroom training, because they can Google or YouTube anything they want from the comfort of their home. In this way they can control when and where they acquire their learning.

Self-directed learning in the workplace is a new and exciting area that caters to companies who want to improve employee development but also acknowledge that everyone learns at their own pace and in their own way. Options could include audio books, videos, and interactive activities, all of which allow employees to work when and where they choose. Traditional workshops cater to a one-size-fits-all approach and by the very nature of big classes and general topics, don't deliver the same value as, say, a much more specific video training.

But, here's the problem: Many organisations don't get it right when it comes to providing learning opportunities to millennials because they think, "Well, this person just joined, they can't expect us to invest in them straight away." Or "They haven't earned that right." Or my all-time favourite, "They have to show us that they are worth that investment." Sounds like a chicken and egg situation. Should leaders wait until millennials have been in the organisation long enough, in order to deserve these learning opportunities? As we already know, millennials are impatient. Waiting is not their MO. If they join an organisation, and start to feel that they are not being valued and there are no development opportunities coming their way, they will be on the first train out! This is why, for millennials, learning should not be based on the amount of time that they have been in the organisation. It needs to be provided in some form the day they enter the workplace.

LEARNING = ENGAGEMENT

Be a proactive leader! Even if the organisation is not big on offering formalised training (at least not for entry level millennials), still find opportunities to help them develop and grow, to hone their skills, to be coached and mentored, to give responsibilities and tasks that allow them to expand their knowledge and experience.

#MindfulMoment

Let's take a breather, literally, and step away from all the traits you must embrace to be a great leader to the millennials. The goal here isn't to overwhelm you with must-dos, but to make you aware that this generation has a lot to offer; however, they view the world from a different perspective. Fair enough! But also to remember that it isn't just how they see the world, but acknowledging that the world is different, and changing rapidly from when we were young. So this little breather is to give you some space to step back and reflect on what you've read so far, and to think about how you can begin to implement a few small changes into your leadership style. Great leaders are not born overnight. Taking baby steps will ensure you get there with your eyes open and your balance mastered.

Mindfulness is a very hot topic these days and we have begun to embrace it in the workplace. At its essence, mindfulness is about being present and aware of where we are and what we are doing in that moment, not thinking of the past or projecting into the future.

How can you, as a leader, use mindfulness for better communication, productivity, and enjoyment? Well, the answer is simple – if you are mindful, then everyone around you benefits. Your calm, focused, reflective, open mind will be contagious.

1 Take a few minutes every day to reflect. Close your office door, take a short walk, or have a coffee and doodle some notes in a special mindful moment notebook.

2 Be present. Focus on the NOW. Where you are right this minute. How you are feeling, what thoughts are going through your head.

3 Use the breath to anchor the mind. Every time your mind goes astray, focus on the inhale and exhale of your breath for a few minutes. Take a deep inhale through your nose, hold your breath for a few seconds, and a long exhale with an open mouth. When your mind is calm, this may lead to a rush of creativity.

"Which world do you want to leave behind?"

Survey respondent

When it comes to millennials, ethics aren't just about youthful idealism, but about a core belief that people and the planet should be treated with respect. The 2018 Deloitte Millennial Survey found that less than half of millennials surveyed believe that businesses behave ethically and are committed to improving society. Their confidence in business is less than that of previous generations, which is why 86 per cent of millennials thought that business success should measure more than just financial performance, and take into consideration things like respecting employees, clients and the environment, integrity and transparency.

Millennials are drawn to companies that contribute to making the world better, are socially conscious, accountable, and have meaningful Corporate Social Responsibility (CSR) programmes. Amongst millennials there is a great concern about issues such as poverty, hunger, the environment, global warming and the importance of sustainability, human rights and education. Companies that do not share these core values of social change would not feature high on the places that millennials want to be employed.

"When I read about companies that operate sweatshops in third-world countries, running multi-million dollar ad campaigns, all I can think is, who do you think you are?"

Survey respondent

According to a study by Cone Communications (2015), 45 per cent of millennials would switch brands to support a cause, 87 per cent would purchase a product with a social or environmental benefit, and 62 per cent are willing to take a pay cut to work for a responsible company.

Climate change, buying locally, giving back to the community, social responsibility and healthy living are all issues that millennials hold close to the heart. This is why companies such as TOMS, who sell ultra-comfortable and trend-setting casual footwear, are so popular. Their marketing platform and corporate value system is all about giving back. Their business model is built on the notion that for every pair of shoes purchased, one is donated. Take a look at their website and you will find a company that is fully engaged in countless social issues from gun control to using art to combat violence. They blog and post on social media. They truly are a company that is in touch with what matters to millennials.

If these guys are so concerned with buying ethical brands and working in organisations that have social impact, this naturally translates into wanting an ethical leader. Who you are and what impact you have will always be more meaningful than what you say.

This trait begs a bit of self-reflection. We all like to think we are good people, but being good requires action, not just sitting on a moral high horse. Pull out a piece of paper and write down a list of your values. They don't have to specifically pertain to the workplace, as our values naturally overflow into all aspects of our life. They define who we are.

A list of possible values:

1 **People should be treated equally regardless of sexual orientation or race**

2 **I believe in being generous whenever possible**

3 **Hard work pays off**

4 **I believe in doing the right thing with integrity and honesty**

5 **You need to be selfish to make money in business**

6 **I tell people what they need to know**

7 **I can do everything alone, no need for team working**

Think deeply about your list and ask yourself if these values fit into society today. Are they ego-centric values or do they embrace a view beyond yourself? Is this the person you want to be? Do your values give you a sense of inner peace or do they add tension to your daily life?

Being a leader means constantly developing your skills, and exploring your own view of yourself, and taking note of how you influence others. Remember, life is a ripple effect - what you believe influences those around you, which influences the world around you.

Once you've taken a look at yourself, ask similar questions of your company.

Project idea: Sit down with a group of millennials at your company and propose a think tank on how you can incorporate change for the better, and change for the future. This might involve:

- *Ethical ad campaign*

- *Teaming up with a local organisation to raise funds*

- *Start a recycling or donation programme*

- *Run the numbers on switching to a more environmentally friendly supplier*

When I was looking for jobs, I received two offers, both in the area of IT engineering, from two different companies. They had similar benefits and compensation as well as flexible working arrangements. So what criterion did I choose to make the final decision? The Corporate Social Responsibility programme of one of the companies! They were involved in projects around health, education, basically investing in human capacity and I thought it was very inspiring. Their programmes were benefitting millions of people in the least developed countries all around the world, and they also gave the staff the option to be involved and volunteer in some of the programmes. It made me feel like I was contributing to a cause that was greater than being just an IT person, and that was the deal-clincher.

Michael, 26,
IT engineer in Berlin, Germany

"Listen, Learn, Participate"

Survey respondent

Millennials want to know their opinions, insights, and knowledge are being heard and count. Much of the disillusionment that millennials face in the workplace is exactly because of this (or rather the lack of this). They are not listened to. They are not asked. So, as you can imagine, they rated strong listening skills as one of the most important traits that they wanted from their leaders.

So what is a good listener?

a) *Someone who nods and makes appropriate facial expressions to indicate engagement, shaking and nodding their head, all the while thinking about what they will have for dinner, or the finer details of date night*

b) *Someone who expertly argues every point made, checks their messages while talking, and never makes eye contact*

c) *Someone who asks what your thoughts are (unprompted) and then takes the time to seriously listen without interrupting, and follows up with questions in order to fully understand*

Well, if you chose c) then you have mastered the skill of Active Listening. If you opted for a) or b), you are not quite there...

I was working on a multi-million-euro international development project and on a short-term assignment to our field office in Turkey. I was in the middle of a funding crisis. Our donors had decided to reduce our funding and we had to prepare three scenario budgets showing the impact the decrease of funding would have. Being the person with the most experience reviewing our budget from HQ, I was thrown into developing all of the necessary budgets. Even though I had never developed budgets before, the project director trusted me to work on the extremely important and time-sensitive budgets. She listened to my inputs and helped direct me so that I would be successful. In the end, I developed several comprehensive budgets and the donors chose the less austere funding option. Because of her allowing me to take on this role, I now have experience developing budgets and am a lot more confident in my Excel abilities. It meant so much to me that she listened to my ideas, and then followed through by being encouraging and paving the way for my success.

Michelle, 25,
project manager at an international
consulting firm in New York, USA

Ernest Hemingway once said:

> **"I have learned a great deal from listening carefully.**
> **Most people never listen."**

We all encounter those people that give a feeble impression that they are listening, but you know they really aren't! They are glancing over your shoulder, checking messages, moving around, avoiding eye contact, tapping the table... You feel the need to cut the topic short because you are wasting their time.

> **"My first supervisor was guilty of this behaviour, and after a while,**
> **her lack of listening skills made me avoid communicating with her.**
> **It caused a great disconnect between us and it also left me feeling**
> **disrespected. Needless to say, it was just a matter of time**
> **until I left the job."**
>
> *Rhonda, 30*

On the other hand, we all recognise those people who are good at listening. We are drawn to them, enjoy sharing our ideas, they allow us time for our stories, and to be ourselves. These are the people who are effective at helping others develop their ideas and talents and solving problems. When someone listens to you, it makes you feel valued and valuable. It's a good feeling that breeds trust. You feel understood. When you are understood, you feel respected. When you are respected, you are more motivated to produce good work. You feel supported. Many could point out that this is obvious. IT IS. Yet so many leaders miss the mark when it comes to effective listening.

Respect is a vital component of listening. When asked what millennials wanted from their leaders, at least 30 per cent of the survey respondents said "respect." What this meant was very simple:

"We respect people who respect us."

Survey respondent

If you respect other people and listen to them, they will respect you back. Active listening improves relationships because stronger connections are created, it helps to build rapport and can dissolve potential conflict that may arise from miscommunication. As a leader, you will never be able to build trust and relationships with your team if you don't practise and learn the art of listening.

In my workplace, we have a lot of young employees in their early 20s and I hear often that they really value transparency and open communication; I recently led a consultation with the whole staff to get feedback on organisational values through a survey and small group discussions to ensure it was an authentic and useful process where people got an opportunity to be heard and contribute - this is pretty unique. We share daily sales results with the whole company, which helps people feel engaged and helps them tie their own work to company results. Taking initiative to do new things or solve problems is highly valued, and as a relatively flat organisation, there is not a lot of bureaucracy to get something from an idea to implementation. It also helps that the CEO listens when any of us have new ideas. I find this entrepreneurial culture really motivating to work in.

Leon, 34,
operations manager in a tech company,
London, United Kingdom

Tips for Active Listening:

- **Give your** UNDIVIDED **attention. Be fully present and mindful when the other person is speaking (no holiday booking, restaurant, or gym routine thoughts)**

- PAUSE **between statements before answering to really think about what is being said**

- OBSERVE **the person's responses and attempt to create a rapport. "Sense and respond" behaviour**

- *Be genuinely INQUISITIVE and CURIOUS, ask questions to clarify and summarise your understanding of the issue*

- *Listen with your BODY. Pay attention to non-verbal signs; face the person, make eye contact*

- *Put your EGO aside. When you are actively listening, the focus is on someone else and you need to take yourself completely out of the equation*

#Emotionalintelligence

"Attitude is a little thing that makes a big difference."

Survey respondent

Emotional Intelligence (EI) is a person's ability to detect and recognise their own feelings and the feelings of others and respond to them in a rational way. In fact, technical expertise was not even ranked among the top traits that millennials wanted from their leaders; it was all the way down at number 10.

Daniel Goleman (mentioned earlier), author of *Working with Emotional Intelligence*, is an expert on the subject. He claims that:

"Emotional intelligence matters twice as much as IQ or technical expertise in determining star performance."

In this hyperconnected world that we live in, most of us have to deal with adversity on a daily basis, so understanding what is happening in your external and internal environment is crucial. Being aware that emotions can drive our behaviour and impact people (both positively and negatively), as well as learning how to manage those emotions – both our own and others' – especially in high pressure environments is a key skill to master.

Consider this scenario:

Over the last few weeks, an employee at our organisation was acting very uncharacteristically, overly sensitive, getting upset very quickly, snapping at colleagues, generally having a bad day (although in his case, it went on for weeks). This was very much in contradiction with his usual friendly and polite demeanour, so it was pretty obvious that something was wrong. At first, his leader pretended nothing was wrong and ignored it, then some days later we noticed that he started to speak to him in a rude and harsh manner, and finally, when he had reached boiling point, he shouted at him in a meeting (in front of other colleagues), "Come on, snap out of it!" This is an example of low emotional intelligence!

How the scenario could have been different if the leader exhibited high EI:

If you sense that someone is emotionally out of sorts, try talking to them in an informal setting. Do not ignore it, or let it linger. Use your communication skills, and try to be a good listener and get to the root of this colleague's uncharacteristic behaviour, which as it turned out was that a close family member was dying. He should have shown a kinder, compassionate approach towards his colleague and empathised with him. And then they could have come up with solutions for the near future on how best to manage the workload while he is going through this stressful phase: hand over some of his work to others, work part time, take some time off to clear his head or spend with family.

This rational, emotionally detached approach to leadership in the workplace may have worked 20 years ago but with the millennials it is not the most effective method for dealing with problems. They want to know that their leaders have their back and that they can count on their support.

Is EI innate or can you develop it?

- *Self-Awareness: Are you aware of your own emotions? Do you take time to self-reflect? Do you examine or assess your emotions? The fact is, most people are so busy in their day-to-day lives that they do not take this time. And it's crucial. Not just for the workplace but in life in general. This means examining how you react to specific situations and how you come across to others. Understand yourself better. Some people can do that by booking a few sessions with a coach, others by stepping out of the routine, taking solo trips, retreats, whatever works for you. It is a crucial part of personal growth.*

- *Self-Regulation: Being aware of emotions is the first step. Second is to monitor your feelings and have control over them (so that they don't have control over you). If you are known as the leader who keeps it calm in stressful situations, this emotional stability will encourage people to trust you. Let's be honest, no one wants to work with or be led by that unpredictable guy!*

- *Social Awareness: Listen. Observe. Understand. With active listening and observation you are better able to empathise with and understand someone else's needs and emotions. Being socially aware means that you have an understanding of the dynamics between people, and can effectively read between the lines.*

- *Social Skills:* *Also known as relationship management. As a leader, have a vision, articulate that vision, and communicate it to your team. Leaders with high EI understand that everyone is different and will therefore adapt their communication style accordingly.*

Good EI enhances relationships, builds stronger communication among people and improves your ability to manage conflict because not only are you in touch with yourself, but you also have an understanding of other people's decisions, needs and desires.

> **"Mastering Emotional Intelligence is the way forward. It will allow you to influence, engage and inspire others."**
> Survey respondent

The following story is a classic case of low emotional intelligence. Imagine if Suzie's CEO did some self-reflection exercises to improve his EI...

A few years ago, I was working for an e-commerce company based in Slovakia, operating online in 15 European countries with around 120 employees. I was responsible for a Slovenian brand of women's lingerie. When I took over, sales were very down, selling 10 pieces a week, which is nothing. Our team did a huge push in terms of promotion, campaigns, working closely on the brand, offering free goodies which customers liked and as a result, sales started to grow to almost 150 pieces sold per week, a huge increase. Keeping track of competition in 15 countries was not an easy task so each country did their own local research and focused on local competition because these couldn't be monitored from the headquarters.

There was this one incident where I came out with a campaign for a new collection of this lingerie brand on Friday. The next day, on Saturday, a team member from one of the local affiliates wrote an email to the CEO of our company to tell him that the biggest competitor of that brand went online with a new collection offering a 70 per cent reduction on their collection that same day. And the reaction of the CEO was shocking. He wrote me a nasty email, copying my immediate supervisor and other senior members of management, blaming me and saying, "Suzie, how will you explain this. If you don't like your job and are not competent to do it then you should pass this brand to someone who can". He lashed out. And as it turned out he didn't even have all the facts; he hardly knew about this brand or its roll-out strategy. When I saw this email I was stunned, frustrated and angry, my whole body was shaking. All my emotions came out. Here I was working day and night to increase the sales of this brand and to do a good job, and this was the thanks I get? I am pretty impulsive as a person, and my first reaction was to hit the reply button and send a nasty email to the CEO with a "Fuck you, don't talk to me that way". Luckily, I calmed myself down. No good comes from taking impulsive reactions, especially in the workplace. I decided not to reply back on Saturday or Sunday. My silence triggered him even more, and I received another few angry emails over the next two days with "I expect your answer right now" and "provide feedback now". By the end of the weekend, the tone had changed from angry to calmer, "Suzie, I look forward to receiving your feedback, please". Clearly he had no awareness of anger management or emotional intelligence. My direct boss who was copied on the messages wrote to me to tell me how sorry she was that I had received these kinds of emails from the CEO, and when I saw that she was on my side, I felt a bit more supported and calm.

I took my time to draft a very long response email that summarised everything about the brand, how it was doing, what has been done since I took it over and addressing that point he had raised of the competition. Actually their portfolio was the same as in previous years, the only thing the competition had done was just use a banner with the 70 per cent discount on it. He would have known that if he had gathered all the information and done the basic homework before humiliating me in front of my supervisor and other peers. I sent the email on Monday, very professional and detailed. I tried not to take it personally and I felt satisfied with myself on how I dealt with the situation and that I did not respond instinctively, as the matter would surely have escalated more. Nevertheless, I had lost trust in the CEO and could no longer take him seriously or look at him in a professional way. I had not had much interaction with him in the past, and I understood after that he was known for his erratic behaviour. He even contacted the suppliers later to tell them what a good job they were doing on this particular brand but not one word to me, either on how well I was doing or apologising for his rude behaviour. It was all-round very demotivating. A year later, the company was bought by external shareholders and as a result most of us were laid off, but by that point I had already been looking for new opportunities.

Suzie, 30,
key account manager at an e-commerce company in Bratislava, Slovakia

"What is your solution?"

Survey respondent

Millennials are known to be dynamic and proactive. They don't want to sit on problems or contemplate them for too long, they want to deal with and resolve them quickly and efficiently.

"The term problem-solving always reminds me of the workplace but overcoming obstacles is something I face every day, whether it's inside or outside the office, it encompasses both my emotional and rational state, it's a much more multi-dimensional approach."

Eliane, 26

Problem solving is passé! It is shoptalk of decades passed referring to isolating a problem and brainstorming solutions. Nothing wrong with that, but as a society we have evolved into a more holistic way of thinking. Not all problems can be solved with crafty solutions. Overcoming obstacles implies a broader and more creative way of dealing with issues, and also allows for the possibility that there isn't a clean-cut solution out there waiting to be discovered, but instead an awareness of the issue, and ways of getting past what is getting in the way. And if there is something that millennials crave, it's creativity, innovation, and thinking outside the box. This is why millennials ranked this as a top trait they want from their leaders.

Following are some questions and prompts that you can reflect on next time you face an obstacle in the workplace, or just take a few minutes to make some notes so you don't feel caught off guard next time a situation gets tense!

Identify the obstacle that you are facing in the workplace.
It could be client-related, a difficult employee, communication problems, lack of motivation....

In what manner will you inform your team about the obstacle?
i.e. a breakfast meeting, during a normal staff meeting, Skype call to everyone – remember, it is better to be inclusive and open, unless the matter is highly personal.

_____
_____
_____
_____
_____
_____

Brainstorm some ways of presenting the obstacle to your team so that it comes across as an issue that can be resolved if you collaborate and work together.

_____
_____
_____
_____
_____
_____

Consider using a technique called *Mind Mapping*. You can do this on a whiteboard or flipchart. Start with a word that represents the obstacle. Write it in the centre of the page and circle it. With the involvement of your team, write down every idea/word that comes to mind. Continue using new words as starting points. Eventually you will begin to see common threads and new ideas and resolutions will emerge.

Anticipate further obstacles that may arise during the meeting, for example someone not offering any suggestions, or giving the impression that this isn't their problem.

_____
_____
_____
_____
_____

Remind yourself of traits that millennials respond to in their leader.

_____
_____
_____
_____
_____

- Millennials are realists and optimistic by nature. They want to know the good, the bad and the ugly of decisions taken. For them, it's the experience and the learning curve that counts. Once a decision has been taken and implemented, they want to know: what did I learn from solving this obstacle? How can I do it better next time? Keep them updated on the progress of projects, be honest about what worked and especially about what didn't. Don't sugar coat the outcomes even if they are not what was expected. It's really about going through the process and coming out the other side with experience, learning and growth. Even if the decision failed, it was an opportunity to learn. Develop a growth mind-set that aspires towards continuous improvement.

- Overcoming obstacles does not only refer to all the logical and rational decision-making that leaders engage in, but also the emotional distress that may be faced, which is why leaders need to have high emotional intelligence so that they can make good decisions in times of adversity and uncertainty. What if two team members become very stressed or agitated at the idea of working Saturdays. Perhaps one has a child, or second job, or an ill family member. Instead of just saying "tough luck buddy, no choice here", let the team know that they can come to you, or speak up during the meeting, and their concerns will be taken seriously.

"Let's have more We, and less Me."

Survey respondent

Sometimes the best ideas are born while doing nothing. Recently I was in a coffee shop waiting for a friend to arrive when I overheard two young men talking quite loudly and enthusiastically. They were clearly students, going on and on about their courses (which were apparently very difficult), their dorm (lots of fun) and the price of drinks (becoming more expensive). As I sipped on my coffee I listened idly. They started talking about their electrical engineering class. Not so interesting, right? Well, one guy was telling the other that a node is that point where all pathways intersect, everything happens here, and if you remove that node, the circuit doesn't work.

My mind started to wander, and then bang, a light-bulb moment. Why couldn't that point where all pathways intersect be a person, a leader in the workplace? A nodal leader. In a technology driven world, a nodal leader would be that person who is the focal point for information flowing to and from different team members, the person who interacts with everyone, is interlinked with the entire team, without whom the circuit would cease to function.

Millennials are big on working together. When the survey respondents answered one of the questions about what message, motto or quote they would put on a billboard in the workplace, more than 30 per cent of the responses were related to the importance of working in teams:

"Strength comes in numbers. Work with people not against them"

"TEAM - Together Everyone Achieves More"

> "There are no boundaries as long as we think and act together"

> "We are a team. Your work affects everyone's day, week, month. Get it done"

> "Together we grow, together we fall"

> "Talent wins games but teamwork wins championships"

Embracing the quality of the nodal leader places you at a centre point from which you can observe what is happening around you. Everyone acknowledges the need for you, yet you are not directly driving the project, because it's the other parts of the circuit that are equally responsible for ensuring that it flows smoothly.

Traditionally, a team leader would be the main person who is assigning the roles and responsibilities and managing the project, dishing out orders to the other members of the team. But this model uses a more bottoms-up approach for leading millennials, which is based on the concept of collaboration, involvement and mutual dialogue, all traits that millennials need to stay inspired in the workplace. In this scenario, the leader still receives and gives information; is present throughout the process; knows when to get involved, contribute, provide guidance, and make suggestions but does so from the side-lines. The team members here are responsible for their own parts in the project, they have ownership, they are involved, and each one contributes to making it a success. In this scenario, the leader has no title.

The nodal leader understands the different team members, their strengths and weaknesses, the team dynamics, how they function, their different perspectives, and provides a safe and comfortable environment where all team members can voice their opinion and ideas without fear of repercussion. At the same time, the nodal leader is responsible for seeing the bigger picture and aligning the goals of the team with the vision of the company, and making sure that the rest of the team is connected and fully aware of that higher purpose as well. That's what makes them the focal point, or the node, in a team or circuit.

> **"It's not about the number of hours worked, but the outcome of your work. We are most productive when we work in teams, not silos."**
> *Ricardo, 30*

One of our survey respondents, Lydia, 30, works for a non-profit organisation that provides additional support for families who have a child on the autism spectrum. The organisation employs several people who work hands-on with the families and are therefore out in the field (in people's homes). Although the office team is small, the roles are very important to keep the organisation running smoothly. There is an administrative assistant, an executive director, two people in accounting, two people in development (funding), and an office manager. Lydia is the development assistant. She told me that she feels very lucky to work in this organisation because there are several young people, weekly meetings where everyone is encouraged to participate, and the executive director is very much like what we described as a nodal leader.

"She obviously has a very important role, maintaining a profile for the organisation, and liaising with politicians, donors, and specialists, but she also oversees the staff. She takes the time to know each one of us, and what our role is. She has said that she trusts and values me enough that she won't micro-manage me. But at the same time she has said her door is always open if I have questions, or suggestions. I can work from home one day a week and on the other days I can work any time between 7 am and 7 pm, so long as my work gets done. It's the best working arrangement for me because I feel part of the team, and she involves me in a lot of the projects and decision-making. I know there is a misconception that if you are part of a team then everyone needs to be present in the office all the time, but really what is the difference so long as you can be reached by phone, email or text? I really appreciate that my company has an open-minded view of teamwork and realises that being part of a team is a mind-set, not a pep rally."

PART IV.

LIGHTS, CAMERA, ACTION

#FindYourChameleon

So now you know what a CHAMELEON leader is, but do you know how to be one? There are dozens, if not hundreds, of leadership models out there but what is often missing are the real-world steps that allow you to put the theory into practice. Read on to find your inner CHAMELEON (not guru-style, adaptable-style!) and take the time to reflect on what traits you already have and which ones could use a tune-up in order to be the leader that millennials want.

LET'S START BY DOING AN ASSESSMENT:

Diagnose
your current leadership realities. How do you rate as a millennial leader?

Understand
where you are RIGHT NOW. Do you already practise some of the required traits?
Are you weak in crucial areas such as communication?
Be open and answer the tough questions.

Pinpoint
what you need to focus on and how you will make changes.

TIPS TO KEEP IN MIND:

- *THOUGHTS: Take a look at the points on the next page and give yourself some quiet time to start the reflection process. Make notes, draw diagrams, make a mind map – whatever it takes to get answers to the tough questions.*

- *REALITY: Mark where you feel you are on the scale of leadership traits. Be honest!*

- *REFLECTION: Ask a few colleagues to fill out the chart with you as the subject. Tell them to be truthful, as you won't benefit from a bunch of "He's a great guy" comments. Look at the responses and see if there are areas where your own answers are very different from your colleagues and think about possible reasons for the variances.*

- *ACTION: Learn how to make change happen.*

- *What causes you stress at work?*

- *Also consider your stress in your personal life. Are you bringing issues to work that are having an impact on your performance?*

- *What are your repeated patterns? Are you doing the same thing over and over again and expecting different results?*

- *What would you say are your leadership weaknesses?*

- *What do you value most in your role as a leader?*

- *Do you have any limiting beliefs or negative thoughts that hold you back?* For example: no one respects me, I'm not qualified for this job, if I had more time I could be a better leader.

- *What gives you energy?*
  This is very important because you can naturally energise yourself and be happier and more effective in the workplace simply by doing more of these tasks.

- *Are you an introvert or an extrovert?*
  If you aren't sure, consider taking the well-known Myers-Briggs test. Introverts tend to recharge their energy by spending time alone whereas extroverts get energy from other people. The opposite could be true, where introverts feel energy being sucked out of them with too much interaction, and extroverts lose energy when they don't have enough interaction.

Some of these questions don't appear to be directly related to being a good leader for millennials, however, by pondering and answering them you will gain a deeper understanding of how you work and where you can focus your energy. A lot of people tend to focus energy on what they are good at, but a certain amount of energy should be directed towards the things that need improvement.

REALITY

Slay!

Damn! I'm
really good!

Mehhh!

Appalling!

Communicate **H**onesty **A**ccountability **M**otivate **E**motional Intelligence **L**isten **E**thical **O**vercome Obstacles **N**odal

Give yourself:
4 points for every **Slay**
3 points for every **Damn! I'm really good**
2 points for every **Mehhh**
1 little point for every **Appalling**

OUTCOME

9-13 POINTS	*Time for a full-length mirror so you can do some serious self-reflection!*
14-26 POINTS	*Kudos! You have some good leadership qualities.*
27-35 POINTS	*Brilliant – all you need to do is sharpen a few skills.*
36 POINTS	*Yasss! You're an EXPERT. Give this book to a friend!*

ACTION

So now you are armed with insightful information. It's one thing to be self-aware and know yourself, but the tough part comes with taking action and making change happen. The first step is to pinpoint exactly what you need to do.

List the CHAMELEON traits where you fall short.

CHAMELEON LEADER - Communicate

Identify 3 of your weaknesses:

_____
_____
_____
_____
_____
_____
_____
_____

Once you have identified the exact issue, brainstorm some solutions for each one.

I avoid face-to-face communication.

Possible solutions:
Tell your team members to remind you when you send an email for something that could more easily be done in person.

_____
_____
_____
_____
_____
_____
_____

Convert your weaknesses to positive action plans:
i.e. Instead of saying, I avoid face-to-face communication, say, If I have the opportunity to communicate face-to-face, or if it saves time, I will do it.

_____
_____
_____
_____
_____
_____
_____

CHAMELEON LEADER - Honesty

Identify 3 of your weaknesses:

_____
_____
_____
_____
_____
_____
_____
_____

Once you have identified the exact issue, brainstorm some solutions for each one.

Possible solutions:

_____
_____
_____
_____
_____
_____
_____
_____

Convert your weaknesses to positive action plans:

_____
_____
_____
_____
_____
_____
_____
_____

CHAMELEON LEADER - Accountability

Identify 3 of your weaknesses:

_____
_____
_____
_____
_____
_____
_____

Once you have identified the exact issue, brainstorm some solutions for each one.

Possible solutions:

_____
_____
_____
_____
_____
_____
_____
_____

Convert your weaknesses to positive action plans:

_____
_____
_____
_____
_____
_____
_____
_____

CHAMELEON LEADER - Motivate

Identify 3 of your weaknesses:

_____
_____
_____
_____
_____
_____
_____

Once you have identified the exact issue, brainstorm some solutions for each one.

Possible solutions:

_____
_____
_____
_____
_____
_____
_____
_____

Convert your weaknesses to positive action plans:

_____
_____
_____
_____
_____
_____
_____

CHAMELEON LEADER - Ethical

Identify 3 of your weaknesses:

_____
_____
_____
_____
_____
_____
_____

Once you have identified the exact issue, brainstorm some solutions for each one.

Possible solutions:

_____
_____
_____
_____
_____
_____
_____
_____

Convert your weaknesses to positive action plans:

_____
_____
_____
_____
_____
_____
_____
_____

CHAMELEON LEADER - Listen

Identify 3 of your weaknesses:

_____
_____
_____
_____
_____
_____
_____
_____

Once you have identified the exact issue, brainstorm some solutions for each one.

Possible solutions:

_____
_____
_____
_____
_____
_____
_____
_____

Convert your weaknesses to positive action plans:

_____
_____
_____
_____
_____
_____
_____
_____

CHAMELEON LEADER - Emotional Intelligence

Identify 3 of your weaknesses:

_____
_____
_____
_____
_____
_____
_____

Once you have identified the exact issue, brainstorm some solutions for each one.

Possible solutions:

_____
_____
_____
_____
_____
_____
_____
_____

Convert your weaknesses to positive action plans:

_____
_____
_____
_____
_____
_____
_____

CHAMELEON LEADER - Overcome Obstacles

Identify 3 of your weaknesses:

_____
_____
_____
_____
_____
_____
_____
_____

Once you have identified the exact issue, brainstorm some solutions for each one.

Possible solutions:

_____
_____
_____
_____
_____
_____
_____
_____

Convert your weaknesses to positive action plans:

_____
_____
_____
_____
_____
_____
_____
_____

CHAMELEON LEADER - Nodal

Identify 3 of your weaknesses:

_____
_____
_____
_____
_____
_____
_____

Once you have identified the exact issue, brainstorm some solutions for each one.

Possible solutions:

_____
_____
_____
_____
_____
_____
_____
_____

Convert your weaknesses to positive action plans:

_____
_____
_____
_____
_____
_____
_____

#HaveAMatchaLatte

So you are loaded with information about millennials and what they desire most from their leaders. But what about the specific millennials on your team? We can't forget the individual in this generation that is so talked about, and so over-categorised. We've focused on what the millennial as a group is all about, and what they are asking for. We've focused on you, the leader, and what traits you should be aware of. We've also focused on the CHAMELEON traits you may need to improve, but now it's time to turn the spotlight on the millennials on your team.

Designate a "Take a millennial for a matcha latte" day. Do it once, or do it once a month. Schedule a coffee out of the office, so you can talk openly and casually. Consider it "a get to know you" session. Certainly don't drill them, or make them feel intimidated; quite the opposite, make them feel important, that you are interested in their opinions about work, politics, family life - let the conversation evolve organically. You can also ask if there is anything they would like to see change at work, or what they think really works well. Basically it is you taking time out of your busy day to listen and learn, and let your millennial know that they are valued.

#LetThemShine

With the job market what it is, lacking security, and millennials jumping around trying to find a good fit that provides both purpose and a place to be valued, there is no doubt that you will find yourself in the position of interviewing one. Remember Maya? She made it very clear that her leader fell short because he didn't listen to her, or take her seriously. She confided in me that her interview process had given her a false impression of the job.

> *"They asked me standard questions like what were my strengths and weaknesses, and what did I think I could bring to the job. But once I was hired, they didn't seem interested in what I could offer outside of the daily routine tasks."*

The interview process is where your leadership begins – this is the first impression they will get of their new leader, and it's important that it's not all about you, but that you reveal yourself as sympathetic, open-minded, team-oriented, and ready to listen as much as talk. They will be evaluating you as much as you judge them, and we now know that they don't tend to take jobs that don't offer real value in return. You aren't doing them a favour by offering them a job, but you will be doing them and yourself a great service by offering an opportunity.

Earlier in the book I mentioned being interviewed by a panel, which had several younger employees present. I was thrilled to be questioned by the very people I would be leading. So how do you turn it around and thrill them to be interviewed by you?

Let them know you are interested in what they have to say. These questions could be:

- *What do you expect from a leader in the workplace?*
- *What is the worst thing a leader could do?*
- *What don't leaders understand about your generation?*
- *Tell me about your ideal workplace.*

Let them know that communication is very important to you as a leader.

- *Tell me about effective forms of communication between leader and team member*
- *Do you value a particular form of communication over others, and why?*
- *Tell me about a communication breakdown that you have experienced. How would you resolve it?*

Before the interview, go through the nine CHAMELEON traits and consider questions around them. Always lead with: This trait is very important to me.

For example: Overcoming obstacles is very important to me as a leader. If we encountered this situation, how would you approach it, and what would you expect my role to be?

Or:

Practising ethical behaviour and actions are important to me. Give me an example of a company that is ethically-minded and what you admire about them. If you can't think of one, suggest a project or policy you would like to see implemented in a company you think falls short in ethical practices.

Being a strong leader for millennials means finding out what is important to them and creating an authentic way to communicate your understanding. This will lead to mutual respect and a happy employee.

#TheNewKidsInTown

As we now live in a world of constant updates, you won't be surprised to hear that millennials are not the latest version. The latest demographic break-downs are Generation Z (GenZ), also known as the "iGeneration" or "Post Millennials". Again, there are a lot of studies about the birth of this generation but most agree that it's late '90s / early 2000s (with some possible overlap with the millennials), so if we are looking at the workplace, these guys have just entered or will be looking for work very soon.

Growing up even more tech-savvy, with an inherently lower attention span but faster processing speed, these young ones like to make an impact, and they don't have patience for things that don't work. Hello, swipe much? Dating on Tinder, posting on Snapchat. Swipe right on your screen for ap-proval, and swipe left to move on. It's that simple. It sounds a bit cold, but really it's not about emotions, it's about efficiency and multitasking. The world is now so full of information, data, choices, messages, and options that this is nothing more than filtering.

Sounds like a great trait to have in the workplace! Think of all the meetings you have sat in where nothing is accomplished. These guys require results, and sitting around talking about shit doesn't get results.

"They are an activist generation, they are not just hashtagging their discon-tent. They are arranging rallies and showing up," (Sinek on Education, Leader-Swipe, July 2019). Perhaps you've heard of Greta Thunberg, the 16-year-old climate change activist who organises protests and reaches people around the globe with her messages.

"Our house is on fire. I am here to say, our house is on fire. [...] I want you to act as you would in a crisis. I want you to act as if our house is on fire. Because it is."

This isn't a book about GenZ so I won't go on about leadership styles with them except to say that they will be demanding a voice. They are team players to the max, they see the world as one place, inhabited by people, not broken down into colours or sexes. They will be at the heels of the millennials in the workplace, and you will have to manage the nudging that will occur.

#JoinTheMovement

So now you can consider yourself in the know! You know what millennials want from their workplace leaders, you know what makes them tick as a generation, and you know the CHAMELEON leadership traits.

Communicate
Honesty
Accountability
Motivate
Ethical
Listen
Emotional Intelligence
Overcome Obstacles
Nodal

You have self-reflected on your own existing skills and come up with a game plan to take action.

Now it's time to join the movement! Millennials love the idea of finding their tribe, their people with like minds and interests that will motivate and inspire them. This sense of belonging and being in tune and understood creates a natural sense of energy that empowers and leads to change. Bring this attitude to the workplace and start a new mind-set of leaders who think young and act wise.

The shift is in place, away from an outdated top-down leadership style to a more inclusive bottoms-up approach. And Millennials want to be included in the leadership process!

Recently I was with a friend and she told me her son was totally into Marvel comics. When she asked him who his favourite superhero is, he said that there wasn't one specifically but he liked it when they all came together to solve a problem because then the world had the benefit of all of their powers.

This is the best message to conclude with: millennials are the superheroes of the future. They strongly believe in coming together and using their unique talents to make the world a better place. Right and wrong isn't something to bend and manipulate, it's just basic black and white: you make a great product, you tell the true story about what it offers, and you treat staff and the customer with respect. It's not about making the most amount of money, it's about creating positive change in the world and being useful.

If you lead them with this in mind, then you will achieve great things together.

Printed in Poland
by Amazon Fulfillment
Poland Sp. z o.o., Wrocław

51071499R00068